Greek Sanctuari

D1461650

The Panathenaic Way crossing the Agora, Athens.
The north face of the Acropolis is in the background.

Greek Sanctuaries

AN INTRODUCTION

Mary Emerson

Bristol Classical Press

This impression 2010
First published in 2007 by
Bristol Classical Press, an imprint of
Gerald Duckworth & Co. Ltd.
90-93 Cowcross Street, London EC1M 6BF
Tel: 020 7490 7300
Fax: 020 7490 0080
info@duckworth-publishers.co.uk
www.ducknet.co.uk

© 2007 by Mary Emerson

All rights reserved. No part of this publication
may be reproduced, stored in a retrieval system, or
transmitted, in any form or by any means, electronic,
mechanical, photocopying, recording or otherwise,
without the prior permission of the publisher.

A catalogue record for this book is available
from the British Library

ISBN 978 1 85399 689 4

Picture credits

American School of Classical Studies at Athens, Agora Excavations: 34, 36, 48, 68, 70, 72
American School of Classical Studies at Athens, Alison Franz Photographic Collection: 1, 6, 9, 13, 14, 17, 19, 20, 22, 28, 30, 32, 38, 40, 41, 42. 43, 46, 50, 51, 53, 55, 56, 60, 61, 62, 64, 67, 71, 74, 77
American School of Classical Studies at Athens: 49, 58, 59
Ares Publishers, inc. (© Jahn/Michaelis): 54
Bridgeman Art Library (© Bibliothèque Nationale Française): 44
British Museum Images © The Trustees of the British Museum: 31, 78
Cambridge University Classical Cast Museum: 8
Deutsches Archäologisches Institut, Athens: 7, 25, 26, 27 [D-DAI-ATH-Acropolis 767, D-DAI-Olympia 174/175, D-DAI-ATH Hege 1847]
Ecole Française à Athènes: 11 (© E. Hansen), 18 (© Y. Rizakis)
Royal Academy: 76
Royal Institute of British Architects: 4, 23

Typeset by Ray Davies

Contents

Preface

Most ancient Greek architecture is in a ruined state. Even the wonderful Athenian Acropolis can seem rather daunting to visitors not provided with a clue to its meaning. The purpose of this short book is to introduce readers to ancient Greek architecture in some detail, and to some extent in its original social and aesthetic context. I hope that it will not only introduce the sites themselves but also open up the wealth of scholarly literature on the subject.

The range of buildings chosen are found in some of the most popular sites and are also those usually set for examination. They are well worth looking at in their own right, and also provide an excellent introduction to other buildings which might be studied later on.

The book is particularly aimed at students who need to understand these buildings in some detail, and who need to be able to use technical language themselves in order to analyse and write about them. Technical language is useful shorthand for discussion purposes; it also is an aid to viewing, helping the eye to interpret and assess what it sees. Students at Sixth Form or High School level will find it useful, as will undergraduates who are new to the study of ancient Greek architecture.

All the translations of Greek passages are my own. The line numbers for poetry are those of the Greek text, so will be close to but not exactly the same as published versions in English. The references for prose passages are to whole paragraphs, so they will match English versions.

I would like to offer my grateful thanks to the many people who have helped me along the way towards producing this book, but especially to Frances van Keuren of the University of Georgia, for her encouragement, criticism and inspiration at an early stage of writing, to Jennifer O'Hagan and Charles Relle, fellow Classicists, for their meticulous and critical reading of the text, to Jan Jordan and Natalia Vogeikoff-Brogan at the American School of Classical Studies in Athens, and to Oliver Pilz of the Deutsches Archäologisches Institut and to Kalliopi Christophi of the Ecole Française à Athènes for their kind and cheerful help with locating pictures, to Zak Emerson for much artistic and technical help with the figures, to Deborah Blake of Duckworth for her support and enthusiasm as well as ironing out of errors, and to Peter Emerson for generous and time-consuming help of all sorts.

List of illustrations

List of illustrations

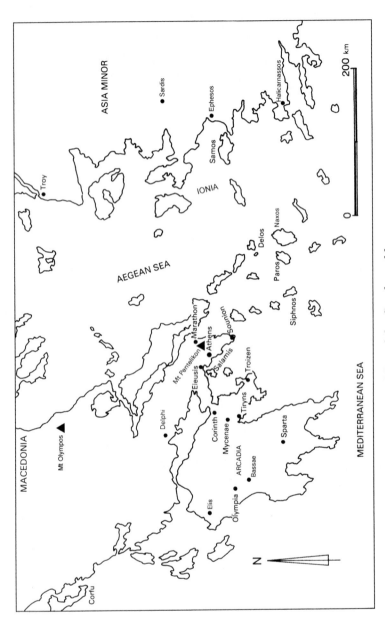

Map of the Greek world

1

Introduction

'Temples of the mind'

The buildings of Delphi, Olympia and the Athenian Acropolis, chosen for study in this book, are 'classics' of Greek architecture: they date from the sixth and fifth centuries BC (the archaic and classical periods). Looking at these few examples in detail provides a useful introduction to the design vocabulary of Greek architecture. Terms explained in the Glossary appear in bold type the first time they are mentioned in the in the text. The book aims to equip the reader to use these technical terms with confidence, and to confront any Greek temple with understanding and pleasure.

There is a great deal of accident in what remains to us of ancient Greek architecture. Most buildings that remain are incomplete and sculptures are fragmentary. Some important temples have left only the scantiest traces or have disappeared completely; the unique architectural aspects of those temples may have vanished, or be traceable only by experts. To appreciate the real character of Greek temples takes some reconstruction work and some imagination. We shall be, as it were, building 'temples of the mind'.

The sameness of Greek temples

A complaint can be made that all Greek temples are the same. Certainly they are all composed of similar elements: steps, platforms, columns, architraves and friezes, pitched roofs and pediments. However, to the interested eye, each temple is unique. Even Doric temples, though said to conform to strict rules, all differ. As in any field of interest, what seems uniform to outsiders is – on inspection – full of nuance, innovation and individuality.

The sameness of Greek temples did not result from lack of imagination; the ancient Greeks are not known for a lack of creativity, so positive causes for sameness should be sought. A building usually declares its purpose by corresponding to a type; a response is aroused in the viewer as a result. A Gothic cathedral for example will be clearly recognisable as such, whatever personal responses a particular viewer brings to it. Another building may 'borrow' a response from the known type: for example, the Houses of Parliament, which were designed with Gothic features in order to 'borrow' the venerability associated with a medieval cathedral.

It is quite normal for building design to contain not only innovation, but also deliberate conformity to a type, sufficient to arouse certain emotional and practical responses from the viewer. There were additional reasons why this conformity should be true of Greek temples. Greeks, while intensely proud of their Greekness, had no political or even geographical unity. What bound them together was cultural: their language, religion, literature, ideas. They were insistent on their 'difference' and their superiority as a group: all others were 'barbarians' – non-Greek-speakers. Greeks lived on the mainland area now called Greece, but also all around the Mediterranean coasts, from Turkey to Sicily, Italy and even France, and on islands (see map). Every city – or **polis** – was self-governing and formed an independent mini-state with the territory around it. The Greek people were not isolated from each other by these great distances but in fact did a lot of travelling, mainly by sea. Trade encouraged constant communication, and so did cultural events such as the four-yearly festivals in the great religious sanctuaries: the Olympic games, the Pythian games and oracle at Delphi, and the lesser games of Nemea and Isthmia.

When worshippers came, for example, from Sicily to Olympia, they would feel quite at home, because the great temple of Zeus would be a supreme example of the kind of temple they expected to see. And the visitor to Sicily would be delighted by the similar temples found there and would also feel perfectly at home. There would be stimulating differences – but no doubt about the shared Greekness.

Landscape

One element, closely bound up with the character of each temple, is less likely to have suffered destruction – its setting. Even the Acropolis in the heart of modern Athens retains much of its natural surroundings, above all, the astonishing rock on which it sits. Delphi, a sanctuary whose site was chosen entirely for the impact of the place itself, retains virtually all its effect for the visitor. Much understanding can be gained from books and photos: yet the physical experience of the place, scents of trodden herbs, sunshine and keen mountain air are unforgettable to the lucky visitor, and are an important dimension of what the designers intended in the first place. In studying Greek temples from a book, this essential element is necessarily missing: the landscape.

The Greeks of our period did not go in for architectural landscaping, that is, they did not alter the landscape setting around their buildings much, as far as we can tell, apart from some planting schemes. They did not carve its contours (as the Romans did) into conformity with their building-plans, levelling hills, bridging gullies and creating straight lines from one area to another. Instead, they were sensitive to what was there already, and placed their buildings to maximum effect, so that nature and art would work together as a satisfying whole. Whether the sanctuary was a local city one or a remote shrine, buildings were planned to accord with the existing contours and character of the site.

Each sanctuary is very different and in fact expresses something of the nature of the god worshipped there: the site fits the deity.

Ancient and modern

Buildings were sited carefully, with reference not only to the view and to near and distant natural elements, but also in relation to other buildings or areas of significance close by. It will make sense to pay attention to these relationships. Most major sanctuaries were built over centuries, so the kind of planning which went into them was gradual and may even appear haphazard. Yet the antiquity of buildings sometimes gave them significance beyond mere appearance. The reverence due to an ancient monument, as with us today, could be played off against the smartness of a new building with interesting effect.

Ancient as the ancient Greeks seem to us, they did not seem so to themselves: they looked back from, say, the fifth century BC to more ancient times with nostalgia and pride in their past as we do, and liked to see it embodied and preserved in ancient monuments. They also liked to add something of their own, in the spirit of their age. Monumental buildings represented cutting-edge art and technology, implied political and military power, and were used to transmit messages about cultural identity. Designers of temples aimed for a physical perfection of beauty, which would speak of divinity and inspire the soul. Patrons wanted to impress visitors with the wealth and sophistication of the city, and to delight the citizens who owned and used the sanctuaries.

2

What was a sanctuary?

This book is about the architecture of the Greek sanctuary, which mainly – though not entirely – means the architecture of Greek temples. We shall be looking in some detail at temple buildings, but also at the layout and function of Greek sanctuaries.

An ancient Greek sanctuary was a marked-out sacred area (**temenos**) where temples – and a range of other specialised structures – might be found. For ancient Greek religion to function, sacred spaces were necessary where people could gather and rituals be celebrated. Rituals varied more than we would expect, including not only religious ceremonies, but also cultural activities such as sport, music events and drama festivals.

Who used sanctuaries?

Those who used the sanctuaries would not have made a particular choice to be religious. A city shrine belonged to the citizen body as a whole; a national shrine existed for all Greeks. Civic religious festivals would be part of a citizen's day-to-day life; participating in them would belong to his identity as a citizen of that city, it would not necessarily be a spiritual choice. Similarly, those who travelled to a more distant sanctuary like Olympia or Delphi were expressing their Greekness and claiming an experience which was theirs by right. There were many facets to the experience, some 'religious', others 'athletic' or 'cultural', some unique to that shrine, others common to all. The sanctuaries we shall be looking at offered ample recreation, a chance for Greeks of widely scattered city-states to mingle and (of special interest for this book) to experience the finest art and architecture available. For a more specifically religious experience, concerning issues of life, death and afterlife, the interested Greek would turn to a mystery religion such as the Eleusinian mysteries, which made special promises and special demands, and for which initiation had to be sought. Such mystery religions were not at all in conflict with civic religion but were additional to it.

What was in a sanctuary?

The most basic elements of a sanctuary were an altar and a boundary (**peribolos**). The altar was essential for the primary act of worship – the animal sacrifice. The boundary separated the sacred area off for its special purpose: dedication to a particular god or gods. Many other ingredients could be in a sanctuary, but these two were absolute requirements.

There might be a visible boundary such as a wall, or a series of boundary stones, or just an understanding of where the boundary was. In a sanctuary of some importance, a monumental gateway (**propylon**) marking the entrance point, the transition from secular to sacred, could heighten the sense of significance. In order for processions of worshippers to reach the altar, a Sacred Way might be planned, or might develop informally over time. The altar would normally be open-air and situated where there was plenty of room for crowds to gather; altars came in many shapes and sizes.

To increase the visible importance of the altar and to house the cult statue, a temple could be added. But the temple was not a necessity as it probably had no particular function in open-air ceremonies. Even a large one was far too small to accommodate the kind of numbers that would attend a public sacrifice. But a fine building would add dignity to a ceremony, and would normally contain the cult image of the god of the sanctuary; opening its doors would allow the god (whose house it was) to see and be seen. A temple could also embody visual messages and so add to the meaning of the sanctuary. It could do this by means of the architecture itself, and also by the sculpted decoration which was part of the design. The building was also intended to delight the viewer by its aesthetic qualities. One of the Greek words for 'statue' is *agalma*, whose literal meaning is 'pleasure' or 'delight'. It was expected that a carved statue would give delight – maybe to the god to whom it was offered, but certainly to its human viewers. By its beauty, a carved temple also justified the enormous trouble and expense of its making.

A temple (normally locked) could serve as a treasury or bank for precious offerings made to the god. This could be a very important function in a rich sanctuary such as the Athenian Acropolis. In a large or complex sanctuary, there would also be individual treasuries: very small – but also eye-catching – temple-like buildings donated by other cities in which to keep their valuable offerings safe.

Any sanctuary would have gradually acquired an large amount of smaller offerings. While buildings would mainly be offered by cities, individuals could make smaller offerings ranging from statues or gold artefacts down to the humblest terracotta figurines or even baby-garments. There are just a few examples of buildings dedicated by very wealthy or powerful individuals. Facilities such as theatres, club-houses, gymnasia and racing tracks were all an integral part of sanctuaries, and the events which they hosted were a part of the religious ritual.

Local or Pan-Hellenic

Sanctuaries were either local or Pan-Hellenic. Local sanctuaries were maintained by a polis mainly for the use of its own citizens, Pan-Hellenic

5

sanctuaries were intended for the use of all Greeks who wished to come, and functioned as meeting places for the Greek community as a whole.

Of the three major sanctuaries we shall be looking at, two were Pan-Hellenic, open to all Greeks. Both were famous for their four-yearly sports events: Olympia held the most important games of all, while Delphi was also famous for its oracle. The Athenian Acropolis was a local sanctuary, primarily intended for the benefit of the people of Athens and its territory, Attica.

Sacred places

Here are two quite well-known passages from Greek drama which describe a 'sacred place'. In the first, Antigone and her old blind father Oedipus have wandered to the outskirts of Athens and stumbled on a shrine. In this case, there was no boundary marked out and Antigone recognises it as a shrine only by its untouched natural beauty.

> This place is holy, as I guess; it bursts
> With laurel, olive, vine; and fluttering
> Around are many sweet-voiced nightingales.
>
> Sophocles, *Oedipus at Colonus* 16-18

Although Antigone recognises the spot as sacred, she does not know to whom. A local person explains:

> All this place is holy ground; awesome
> Poseidon dwells here; and the divine fire-bringer
> Titan Prometheus; the spot you stand on
> Is called the Brazen Threshold of this land
> Bulwark of Athens; and the neighbouring fields
> Claim for themselves this horseman as their leader,
> His name to be their own – Colonus ...
>
> Sophocles, *Oedipus at Colonus* 54-9

A sanctuary can be dedicated to multiple deities and heroes, some of major importance such as Poseidon, and some never heard of outside their own village, like Colonus.

In the next example, Socrates has taken an unaccustomed (for him) walk outside the city. He recognises the place as special by the same kind of natural features as Antigone noticed, this time including water. For him, what clinches it as sacred is the man-made evidence – the statues and other votive offerings, proof of worship.

> By Hera, what a lovely place to stop! This plane tree so spreading and high, and the lovely shadiness of the willow ... in full bloom, it makes the place so fragrant. And besides, the spring is really charming, the way it flows from under the plane tree – very cold water judging by my foot! The place seems

6

to be sacred to the Nymphs and to Achelous because of all the statues of girls and the other votive offerings. And ... how pleasant and sweet the fresh air ... Clear and summery, it is humming with the chorus of cicadas. But the nicest thing of all is the grass, the way it grows on a gentle slope, thick enough to be just right when you lay your head on it. (Plato, *Phaedrus* B-C)

The sacred place seems to be what we would call a beauty spot. The natural elements come together in a way that particularly impresses the viewer. In both of these examples the response of the visitor is actually to sit and enjoy the place.

Mountains, caves, groves, springs: these were the kind of natural features which attracted worship. There was a sense of the numinous – that is, a feeling that the place was somehow haunted by an unseen unexplained spirit. In the shrines we shall look at, built up and sophisticated as they were, it is still possible to sense the special natural character that had first attracted this kind of attention.

3

From mud hut to marble temple:
Doric and Ionic

Predecessors

The origins of Greek architectural style are much studied yet remain obscure. What seems clear is that monumental buildings entirely of carved stone in recognisable architectural style began to be built around the beginning of the sixth century BC. As we shall see, there were basically two styles: **Doric**, a plain and sturdy style developed first; **Ionic**, more graceful and decorative, soon followed.

At that time, Greeks would have had some notion of monumental stone buildings in Greece from the still visible remains of masonry dating from the Bronze Age, or, as they would have called it, the Age of Heroes. Impressive architectural ruins were to be seen at Mycenae, with its monumental Lion Gate, and elsewhere, some of which are still visible today (Fig. 1). The walls of these ruins are composed of enormous boulders, roughly shaped and fitted together, held in place by gravity, small pieces of rock stuffed into any gaps. **Cyclopean** fortification walls of this date were still in use in the early fifth century on the Acropolis of Athens.

However, with the collapse of Mycenaean civilisation (*c.* 1200-1100 BC), knowledge of how to make buildings of massive stone seems to have been lost for several centuries. During this period walls were made of mud-brick or wattle-and-daub and roofs of thatch, with wood as a framework. Unbaked mud reinforced with straw and hair can be shaped in moulds into large rectangular blocks that fit together neatly. When kept fairly dry, but not too dry, mud is a strong and durable material; however, it dissolves in water. This factor would dictate such safety measures as overhanging roofs, protective surfaces and stone rubble foundations. For extra strength and protection from damp, stone could be used in lower courses of walls, and little cylinders of stone might be used as bases for wooden columns. Such building methods are obvious ways of using readily available materials; they were used by the Greeks for buildings of every size, during what are called the Dark Ages between the Mycenaean era and the sixth century BC. Even after the introduction of stone and marble for temples, these perishable materials continued to be used for private houses and humbler public buildings. Such buildings disappear leaving little apparent trace, yet archaeologists can detect, and, to some extent, reconstruct them.

3. From mud hut to marble temple: Doric and Ionic

1. The Lion Gate at Mycenae, *c.* 1250 BC.

'Dark Age' temple building

It is thought that Mycenaeans did not build temples, but worshipped in open-air sacred areas around an altar, or else incorporated shrines into the palace-buildings that characterised their civilisation. Homer, writing *c.* 750 BC, mentions a temple on the Trojan citadel containing a seated statue of a goddess (*Iliad* 6.300). Though the poet may have pictured his Trojan temple among palaces 'of polished stone', real temples throughout the so-called Dark Ages (*c.* 1100-600 BC) were probably made of wood, thatch and mud with some use of stone for foundations.

The ground plans of such wood-framed buildings have been traced. The construction method and materials limit the width (because wooden beams were needed to span the roof, whether flat or pitched) but do not

9

limit the length; it would be easy to add extra rooms or sections by elongation. On a large-scale building, the pitched roof would need a central internal row of columns as support, probably reaching up to the ridge beam. The thatch would lend itself well to a rounded apse-end at the rear. However, at the front, the face of the pitched roof would be a flat triangular gable-end, perhaps left open for a smoke-outlet. Additionally, a porch could be added to protect the entrance, and an all-round colonnade could support the overhanging roof. The overhang, having begun as a protective measure for mud walls, would then become a useful shaded space for social activity. The wooden props to support the overhang would not need to be very strong or very close together.

Evidence for buildings of this sort is also found in the form of eighth-century painted terracotta models (two are displayed in the National Archaeological Museum, Athens) which feature the steep apse-ended roof, apparently thatched, the open triangular gable front, and the porch with slim, apparently wooden columns.

Changes came with the invention of terracotta roof-tiles to replace thatch. The enormous weight of a tiled roof made more demands on the sub-structure, so the wooden elements would need to become more massive. In addition, tiles – which are held on a roof largely by gravity – need to lie at a shallower angle than thatch – which requires a steep pitch for run-off of water. Tiles also fit more easily into a rectangular arrangement, so the apse-end would become out-dated.

Some elaborate temples were built using terracotta to protect, and then to decorate, the exterior wooden parts of the structure. Terracotta could easily be painted and moulded. An example of this was the wooden temple of Apollo at Thermon dated to the late seventh century, which had impressive roof ornaments in painted baked clay and a set of painted clay panels as well (also in the National Archaeological Museum, Athens). A conjectural reconstruction of this building suggests a fairly finished Doric form, realised in wood and terracotta.

Stone-working

An essential factor in the move toward stone-building was the discovery of stone-working skills. Monumental sculpture began to appear in the mid-seventh century. Masonry and sculptural skills overlap and both were necessary if stone architecture was to be developed. All elements of a stone building, whether decorative or 'plain', had to be hand-carved. It cannot be emphasised enough that the high precision carving of a Greek temple is a large part of its aesthetic effect. The joints, if visible, are planned, not randomly placed. On the whole, they are so precise that they can hardly be seen. Every block fitted a particular position on the temple; they were not interchangeable. This fine fit was to a large extent what kept the building together, since no mortar was used. This is why a collapsed temple can be successfully re-erected.

3. From mud hut to marble temple: Doric and Ionic

The development of stone sculpture might in itself have influenced temple design. A cult statue would lose some of its visual impact when placed to the side of a central row of columns; a central position between two framing rows of columns would provide a more dramatic focus. The double row of columns would then suggest or require a more complicated roof structure, involving horizontal cross-beams (Fig. 27). These beams would increase the stability of the whole structure, and the idea of a horizontal ceiling could then naturally develop, filling in between the beams, closing off and hiding the roof-space. The ceiling could then eventually become a decorative feature in itself.

'Petrification' of wooden forms

It is broadly agreed that the forms of the wood, mud and tile temples were converted into carved stone. The details of this process are far from clear.

As we saw earlier, it was desirable for temples to be easily recognised as such. Since they had no function other than to house a statue and to indicate the 'presence' of a god, their appearance and the impression they created were the most important thing about them.

Stone was a far more impressive and durable material than mud and wood or even than painted moulded terracotta. The idea of carved stone buildings must have been derived from the disciplined architecture of Egypt (where Greeks were first allowed to settle in mid-seventh century) as well as from Asia Minor, with perhaps some inspiration from the rugged stonework of the Greek heroic age (Mycenae, etc). Stone buildings making use of columns, decorative carving and impressive statues were to be seen widely in Egypt. Luckily for the Greeks, their local **limestone** and subsequently marble lent themselves to fine and fluid carving very readily, unlike the hard granite of Egypt.

The move to stone necessitated much more serious foundations to bear the great weight. A wood and mud building might make use of stone rubble for foundations under the weight-bearing sections, and make do with beaten earth for the floor. But the solid platforms on which stone temples are raised have the double benefit of displaying the temple and of providing a firm basis of finely-fitting squared blocks which hold together well in an earthquake. Under the more weight-bearing sections, ie the walls and the colonnades, the stone foundations go deeper (Fig. 27).

In the pre-stone temples, colonnades were of wood. Wooden columns could be thin props or whole tree trunks, shaped with an axe. It is speculated that either the natural tree-shape or the downward strokes of the axe on a rounded trunk could have given rise to the downward grooves on Greek stone columns, termed **fluting**. To support the enormous weight of a stone and tile roof structure, columns had to be both sturdy and carefully spaced. Engineering calculations would be made as to size and closeness of supports for the weight-bearing stone beams that lay across

11

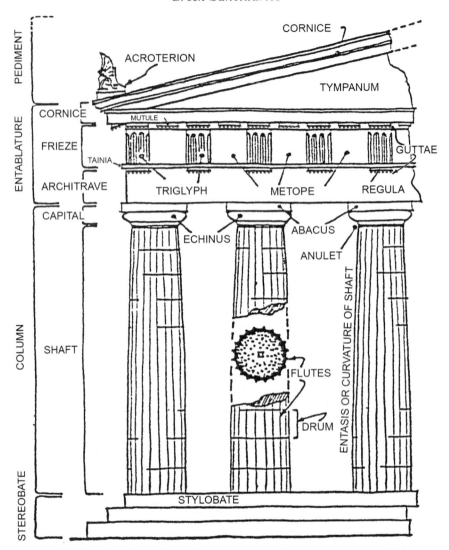

2. Drawing of a Doric elevation.

them; an appearance of combined strength and ease was desirable. Such calculations led eventually to the complex and subtle system of proportions which characterises Greek architecture, and which goes way beyond practical necessity.

While a wooden structure would hold together by means of joinery, a stone structure relied a great deal on gravity. The structural method of a Greek temple is known as post and lintel, meaning that horizontal members rest upon vertical props. The simplest example of this method is

Stonehenge, where it is easy to see the principle at work. The weight, if fully supported, actually holds the structure together. This method of building continued unchanged for centuries among the Greeks, just being refined in details. It was the Romans who took classical architecture finally in new directions with their exploitation of the arch, **pier**, and vault, the decorative column and the use of concrete.

Use of materials

Stone columns were at first **monolithic**, i.e. made from a single block. Later it was found more practical to fit together several **drums**, giving the effect of a single block; together they made up the shaft. At the top of the shaft was the **capital**, a crowning element, which was broader and spread the weight of the superstructure more widely. This extra section became decorative and gave character to the building. Upon it rested the heavy horizontal beam (**architrave**), with another beam above (fronted by the decorative **frieze**); they supported the roof-structure. The roof was pitched, that is, it consisted of two slopes resting against each other at the high **ridge**, leaving at each end a triangular space which was filled in with an upright wall (**tympanum**), or gable end. This triangle is the pediment, which, together with the colonnade, is a 'trademark' element of classical architecture (Fig. 2).

Even in a stone temple, the hidden parts of the roof were usually constructed of wood. This would lighten the heavy load a bit. Roof tiles would be terracotta or marble. Everything else would be of stone except the interior ceiling and the doors. The ceiling would be made in a complicated 'box' construction called **coffering** which would be realised in wood indoors (Fig. 70), and in stone in the covered colonnade area. The doors would be made of imported wood: ebony, cypress or cedar of Lebanon, with inlay of ivory, metal or other precious material. Wood was not necessarily a cheap alternative for the Greeks, since suitable timber was not plentiful. Pine might be imported from Macedonia or the Black Sea for general carpentry, and the exotic showy woods from the Southern Mediterranean.

The stone for a temple was usually local for the sake of cheapness. But very often the sculptured parts would be of marble imported from the Cycladic islands, probably Naxos or Paros. **Parian** was the favourite because of its pure white brilliance, while **Naxian** was greyer. In Athens, after about the first quarter of the fifth century, the local **Pentelic** marble was used. Having this readily available fine material, Athens had a natural advantage

The provision of stone, whether imported or local, was a complicated process. It had to be ordered well beforehand in specific sizes to be quarried by skilled workers, then roughly shaped at the quarry to reduce the bulk for transport. Labour and transport were vital elements of cost in the planning of a temple.

The Greek architectural orders

There are two main styles in ancient Greek architecture: they are known as the Doric and Ionic orders. Doric is associated with the Greek mainland while Ionic originates from Ionia, Greek city-states of the islands and eastern coast of the Aegean. Doric is considered to be sturdy, 'masculine', rule-based, uniform. Ionic is considered to be elegant, 'feminine', decorative, inventive. These are of course stereotypes. The two styles have plenty in common.

Doric ground plan

Study of a ground plan of a Doric temple will show that the peripheral part of the roofed area is open-air (Fig. 3). The relatively small indoor part, enclosed by walls, is the **cella** or **naos**. It was lockable and contained the statue, and perhaps precious offerings too. Access was controlled, and the small size of the cella or naos did not matter since worship took place outside, and was focussed on processions and sacrifices.

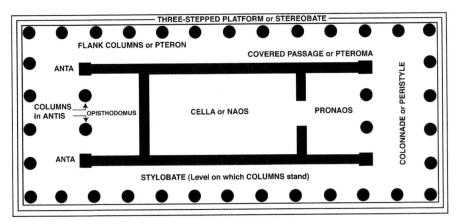

3. Ground plan of a Doric temple.

The ground plan of a temple or treasury is simple, not so different from the Dark Age hall, except that measurement and proportion become ever more calculated and sophisticated. The cella is an enclosed, rectangular, roofed chamber, usually single, sometimes double. It may be surrounded by a colonnade or **peristyle** on a raised platform, reached by steps. There will probably be a porch at the entrance (**pronaos**) and perhaps a matching porch at the other end (**opisthodomos**). Porches are defined by the protruding ends of the cella walls and these protruding sections are called **antae**. Porch columns may be arranged between the antae: **in antis**. Or they may be more numerous and spread right across the façade: **prostyle**.

3. From mud hut to marble temple: Doric and Ionic

Doric style

Doric is characterised by its columns and its frieze (Fig. 2). The pediment is common to both orders, Doric and Ionic. Doric columns are tapered and fluted; that is, the shaft is wider at the bottom than at the top, and is carved with shallow concave grooves running downwards which meet at sharp vertical ridges called **arrises**. The columns sit firmly on the **stylobate** or top step of the platform (**stereobate**), with no separate base or other element. The join with the platform is elegant and economical. The capitals consist of two sections, a cushion-like circular lower section (**echinus**) which supports a square flattish element above (**abacus**). On this sit the architrave and frieze, two horizontal beams which, together with the decorative projecting **cornice** above, make up the **entablature**. Below the echinus are some unobtrusive rings around the thinnest part of the column: these are necking rings or **anulets**. The square abacus juts slightly beyond the architrave which rests on it. Since the column foot aligns with the edge of the platform, it is easy to see that the abacus is slightly more spreading than the column shaft at its widest part. The column, as well as tapering overall from bottom to top, usually has a feature called **entasis**: this is a slight swelling towards the middle of the shaft, more pronounced in the sixth-century archaic period, and more subtle in the fifth-century classical period.

Above the plain architrave is the **Doric frieze**, a horizontal band of decoration divided into alternate sections – **metopes** and **triglyphs**, both roughly square. Triglyphs are divided vertically into three strips divided by two carved grooves (and normally two half-grooves on the edges), hence the name. Metopes are slightly recessed flat plaques which can be painted or carved with mythological figures. Below the frieze runs a thin projection called a **tainia** or 'ribbon'. Above and below the frieze are some strange features with the appearance of blocks with pegs sticking out of them. They are arranged at regular intervals: under each triglyph, a thin **regula** with peg-like **guttae** adheres to the tainia; and above every metope and triglyph, a **mutule** adheres to the bottom surface of the cornice (**soffit**); it looks like a larger block, from which two or three rows of little 'pegs' can be seen hanging down. These features have such a utilitarian appearance that the conviction arises that they are functional wooden structures copied in stone. They have no function in the stone system of the Doric order, yet are an invariable part of the Doric frieze (Fig. 38).

The metopes and triglyphs arouse similar discussion. Vitruvius, the first-century AD Roman architectural writer, derived the triglyph form from the wooden roof beam-ends resting on the architrave. The triglyph grooves would be a reminder of the rough natural texture of the cut wood; the metopes would be plain or decorative slabs masking the spaces between. While this explanation holds quite well for the frieze running along the bottom of the sloping roof, it makes no sense on the façade under the

15

pediment, where no beams would end. But these functional-looking forms probably became conventionalised, retaining only a distant relationship to any real structural parts.

Another reminiscence of wooden forms is the thickened anta. The antae are the extensions of the cella walls which form the porch area. When the walls were made of mud brick, these sections were vulnerable to damage and so were cased in wooden planking. This thicker casing is copied in stone.

The cella walls also reflect the old mud brick construction. Mud brick could rest on a lower course of worked stone which lifted it away from the harmful damp of the ground. The lowest few feet of an **ashlar** wall are often differentiated with a taller course of blocks called **orthostates**. These preserve tradition and also look good – the base of the wall is emphasised and appears strong.

Another mud-brick feature was the gradual tapering of the wall towards the top: this is sometimes imitated in stone.

Ionic style

The Ionic order is also distinguished by its columns and its frieze (Fig. 54). The columns are typically tall and slender. They may taper only slightly and will probably not have the faint curve (entasis) of Doric. They stand upon fairly elaborate bases. In the old wood and mud construction, stone bases had served the practical purpose of protecting wooden columns from rotting at the bottom, especially when standing on an earth floor. While Doric abandoned this feature, Ionic developed it. Varied 'rings' of convex and concave sections were piled into an interesting shape (Fig. 52). On a grand temple, such as that of Artemis at Ephesus, the column-shaft just above the base might even be sculpted with narrative.

The Ionic capital is the most eye-catching feature of the order (Fig. 4). Like the Doric capital, it has an abacus and an echinus. But the abacus is so small it is hardly noticed – while the echinus is prolonged into two delightful scrolls (**volutes**) curling down; a decorative band fills the space between.

The flutes of the Ionic column are also more elaborate than the Doric and there are more of them on a slimmer shaft. The ends of the vertical grooves are rounded, top and bottom; between the grooves are flat sections called **fillets**. As the shaft meets its base, it is likely to flare out slightly, unlike the Doric, which maintains its steady simple line. The Ionic column is elegant but definitely 'busier' than the Doric.

The entablature resting on the columns will be divided as before into architrave and frieze with cornice above. The architrave will probably be divided into three plain steps, imitating overlapping wooden boarding. The frieze will be continuous and may be topped with a carved **dentil** design of alternating tooth-like blocks and spaces (Fig. 66). These perhaps

4. Engraving of an Ionic capital from the Erechtheion, Athens.

represent the small roof rafters, just as the triglyphs represent the heavier beam-ends. In Ionia, the frieze itself will be left plain or even omitted; on the Greek mainland a sculptured narrative often replaced the dentils. Similarly, the Ionic pediment was usually left empty in Ionia, but often sculpted in mainland Greece.

The examples of Ionic style examined in this book will all be mainland ones, and display a certain Doric influence. Ionic temples in their homeland of Ionia are often very vast, so much so that they may even be unroofed in the central area. While the elements used are similar to Doric, the effect must have been very different indeed.

Major Ionic temples in East Greece

The important temple of Hera on Samos (38 x 85 metres), built in the last quarter of the sixth century, illustrates Ionic layout (Fig. 5). Its restored ground plan shows that it was **dipteral** on the flanks, i.e. the colonnades are two deep. On the short ends, it was **tripteral**, i.e. there was a third row of columns. At the back end, these rows were of nine columns each, uniformly spaced. On the entrance front, the rows were of eight columns each, and the spacing varied, being wider at the centre; this was achieved by removing a notional central column and then readjusting the spacing of the central four. This more open front arrangement threw a strong emphasis onto the entrance. Through the three rows of porch columns could be seen inner depths – the extended antae enclosed two smaller-scaled colonnades of five each side, leading to the door itself. Overall, the effect would have been of a 'forest of columns' – it is speculated that a temple like this was even intended to recall a sacred grove. Furthermore, the emphasis was on the front and the entrance, whereas a Doric temple did not draw special attention to its entrance.

The varied spacing of Ionic façade columns just described was easily achieved because of the flexibility of the continuous frieze above. The disciplined arrangement of the Doric triglyph frieze encouraged much greater regularity in spacing. Nevertheless, it will be seen that the great Ionic temples of the east had a certain influence on mainland Doric, mostly at Athens.

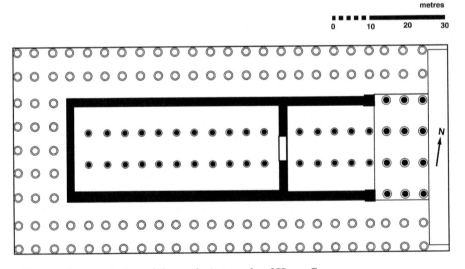

5. Restored ground plan of the archaic temple of Hera, Samos.

4

Architectural sculpture

Architectural sculpture is often studied out of context. This approach is prompted and reinforced by the fact that very little architectural sculpture remains in situ. The typical location for admiring such works is in a gallery or museum where they appear as relief or free-standing sculptures in their own right, studied for their place in the evolution of sculptural style as a whole. Here, we shall consider architectural sculpture only in its intended role as part of a building.

Architectural sculpture in its original context can be viewed formally as a way for the designer to highlight particular parts of a building; or it can be seen iconographically as a vehicle for specific messages, interpreting or reinforcing the meaning of a building. In both aspects, it should be seen as an integral part of the architecture. Equally, we can reverse the idea: since every inch of a Greek temple or treasury was skilfully carved and shaped with sculpting techniques to fit a unique slot in the whole, we could view the entire building as a complex piece of sculpture, combining both abstract and organic forms.

Sculptured components of a temple

The buildings we will be considering are for the most part temples and treasuries (which have the form of miniature temples). The buildings vary but, as we have seen already, are made up of similar components: a stepped platform, columns supporting an architrave topped by a frieze, a cornice and a pediment. Originally the three corners of the pediment were finished with roof sculptures (**acroteria**): these tend to be forgotten as there are none left in situ to remind us of their position; and there was further decoration along the roof edge on the flanks (Figs 2, 36).

The areas on the building where we can expect to see major sculpture are the triangular pediments, the rectangular metopes (if the frieze is Doric) or the long ribbon of the continuous **Ionic frieze**. Each building differs in the amount of sculpture it carries and on which of the likely areas of the building it is found; this is a design point to which the ancient viewer would have been immediately sensitive.

The Greeks were very conscious of structures and the structural components of a complex whole. Temples come in all sizes, yet the elements and their proportions are constant. Sculptures on a temple always emphasise the component parts.

Doric decoration

In a Doric temple, the pediment is likely to be the major focus. Second to that, the viewer will check the metopes. If the pediment is empty, more emphasis will fall on the metopes, or vice versa. The viewer might also check the inner porches for a second sculptural sequence, especially if the outer metopes were blank (Figs 25, 26).

The platform and columns of a Doric temple remained undecorated. Since columns were fluted, this was considered decoration enough: no one would want to interfere with the pure vertical sweep of the column with its subtle curve from pavement to entablature. However, the Doric capitals and anulets, though plainly carved, were marked out with paint.

Above the capitals comes the architrave, topped by the frieze. The Doric frieze is divided into triglyphs and metopes. The metopes, whether sculpted or not, would have been picked out with paint. The horizontal of the frieze is therefore always emphasised by these decorative segments, which partly interrupt the horizontal with groups of mini-verticals (the triglyphs), echoing the fluted columns.

At each narrow end of the building rises the triangular pediment. In a Doric temple of any importance, this will probably carry sculpture. In any case, there is a nice geometric contrast of the elongated flattened triangle with the rectangular building it crowns. As mentioned above, the pediment will usually be punctuated by acroteria on the central peak and at each corner. These will obviously vary in size in accordance with the building's size and may therefore be enormous or quite small. Acroteria are often in the form of winged or wind-swept figures because they are viewed against the sky; or for the same reason they may be elaborate floral motifs with a pierced design through which light shows.

Meanwhile the side view of the building was routinely enriched with a decorative **sima** or gutter, lion-head waterspouts or rows of decorative **antefixes** edging each line of tiles where they end above the architrave. These will be marble if the tiles are marble or sometimes terracotta if the tiles are terracotta.

The typical three-quarter view of a temple will include all of this decoration, both front and side. This may well be why Doric temples are often placed obliquely to their approach path – for example, the initial view of the Parthenon – instead of head-on as we might expect (Fig. 36).

Ionic decoration

The Ionic order (Fig. 54), while similarly furnished with columns and pediments, differs in emphasis. In Ionia, the Ionic pediment was normally left empty, though the borders were probably decorated. The frieze might be topped with dentils but will probably not be carved. However, in mainland Greece, Ionic pediments and friezes are very likely to be carved, through the influence of Doric style. The capitals are of course very decorative and varied with their volutes and other ornaments. The slender shafts are fluted more elaborately and have bases with more or less elaborate mouldings. Steps will be undercut. There will be more mouldings, and border patterns may be richly carved where Doric would make do with paint. Overall, the effect is lighter and the decorative carving is spread more evenly over the whole, while Doric concentrates attention around the entablature.

The Ionic order retains the key elements of column and pediment, but is allowed to aim at more dazzling effects. Thus, the sequence of elements is less inevitable than the Doric. There may be more surprise, more variation or more profusion: as we have seen, the great Ionic temples of Ionia could duplicate colonnades till the eye must have been confused and amazed. Ionic style could also vary its spacings and play with the ideas of interior and exterior. Interiors were sometimes unroofed, a grove might be growing there with perhaps another smaller temple inside the grove. Therefore the viewer of an Ionic temple might have approached with a more open mind where the viewer of Doric might be more sure of his expectations.

Colour

The use of colour is easily forgotten when imagining the original effect of Greek art and architecture. There is plenty of evidence that it was there, but attempts to reproduce it look crude. Red and blue were the major colours, with black, white, yellow and some green. Gold leaf was used, too. Sculpture, including of course the figures in friezes, metopes and pediments, would have had realistic facial details added in paint, and could be enhanced with gilded bronze accessories; coloured robes or painted borders emphasised the forms of drapery (Fig. 6). On a building, it seems likely that red or blue backgrounds marked out the main architectural formatting: for example, the tympanum of a pediment, the long friezes, the thin horizontal **tainia**, and so on, while triglyphs and metopes would have alternated red and blue. Uncarved Doric architraves and cornices would have carried painted patterned borders, similar to those on drapery. Ceiling coffers of marble or wood were also painted and gilded. All of this detail would have helped the eye both to assimilate the geometric forms of a building, and to identify the sculptural narratives, since the figures would have stood out clearly against the solid-colour background. The colour might also have relieved the glare of the sun on marble buildings of freshly-cut whiteness.

Both orders were decorated with colour in this way. It can be seen from the above that, though Doric is considered to be the 'plain' order of Greek architecture, it would actually have been rich and lively with plenty of interest for the eye. The overall effect was sturdiness and strength below, with strong colour effects above, while Ionic was jewel-like throughout.

21

6. Archaic kore with preserved painted detail, *c.* 530-520 BC, Acropolis Museum, Athens.

An early archaic Doric pediment: the temple of Artemis at Corcyra

Coming to specific examples of architectural sculpture, we find that the first known stone-carved temple in Greece not only carries its full complement of Doric detail with guttae, mutules, etc, but also has a pediment fully sculpted in limestone. This is the **octostyle** temple of Artemis at Corcyra (Corfu) dated *c.* 580 BC.

This early archaic pediment (Fig. 7) is sometimes treated dismissively as 'primitive', yet it already displays some of the ongoing

7. Reconstruction drawing of the 'Gorgon pediment', temple of Artemis, Corfu, *c.* 580 BC.

8. Gorgon, cast of detail of pediment, temple of Artemis, Corfu, *c.* 580 BC.

characteristics of pedimental design. The most obvious is symmetry, together with conformity of the design to the triangular field. The symmetry is not precise but is dominant: the most prominent section is the central winged Gorgon who faces frontally but races towards the viewer's right; the largest area is taken up by the mirror-image pair of flanking leopards. There are also two smaller narrative scenes placed, one at each corner, where the pediment narrows. Interest carries right to the extremities and all the figures are adjusted to the available space, though not uniform in scale.

Limestone is more difficult to carve successfully than marble because the texture is rougher. The sculptors of this piece have achieved a surprising degree of fine detail, for example Medusa's ringlets (Fig. 8). They also used undercutting, i.e. a little stone is cut from underneath and behind the figures, creating very strong shadows. This makes the figures seem separate from the background with a life of their own. Medusa herself is in a primitive kneeling-running position, and her head overlaps the confining decorative border at the apex so that she can be understood to be bursting dynamically out of the pediment towards the viewer. The spots on the leopards are lightly outlined, so we can deduce brightly coloured spots on them and bright colour on the Gorgon too, especially her hideous lolling tongue. In the right-hand corner, Zeus battles Giants and Titans in his early struggle for supreme power. He is small but deeply carved; parts of him are almost completely freestanding from the background.

The whole scene, despite the inconsistency of scale, can easily be read as a thematic illustration of divine power at work, offering both protection and a warning. The powerful Medusa is alive and well, sheltering her two children, Chrysaor and Pegasus. This adds a political dimension since Corinth, (the mainland city which planted the colony at Corcyra), often used the winged horse Pegasus as an emblem.

So in this earliest example of a pedimental sculpture, we already find:

- An intriguing tension between the confining geometric format and the exuberant liveliness of the figures. Although these figures are in the stiff early archaic style, the sculptor has made a real effort to suggest that they are capable of independent life away from their limestone background. Pure geometry confines organic figures that are constantly on the verge of escape.
- Concern for balance and symmetry, combined with dramatic narrative.
- Themes which have both 'theological' and political reference.
- Decorative forms which would certainly have shown up clearly and effectively from a distance and were designed to do so.

All these design principles will be carried forward throughout the development of architectural sculpture.

Delphi

Apollo was the god of Delphi and lord of the oracle. By killing the resident dragon, Pytho, he had won for himself the title 'Pythian', which also was given to the prophetess and the quadrennial festivals.

The site seems to have been continuously active from about the tenth century BC, the oracle by the eighth century, but the Pythian games only from about the early sixth century. They were not as old as those of Olympia and came second in importance. However, Delphi will be dealt with first, because of the age and influence of its main temple and some of its other buildings.

The landscape

Many sanctuaries are remarkable for their natural setting, but Delphi must be the most dramatic of all (Fig. 9). Placed high on a steep mountainside where the terrain has to be steeply terraced for building, the site is difficult to reach. However, it also has amazing advantages. The air is keen and bracing. The view is stunning and far-reaching. Just to be at Delphi feels like a spiritual experience, where the mind grows sharper, the outlook clearer.

Views are varied and varying: to the south a vast and open panorama of usually blue mountains and sun-filled green valley far below. To the north – and very close – the sheer rock face of the Phaidriades ('Shining ones'), and the twin peaks of Mount Parnassos. These cliffs and crags are dark and ominous, not quite as shining as their name suggests, and they loom upwards, pathless, inaccessible.

These two aspects reflect the many-sided Apollo. He is the sun-god and patron of music, harmony, rationality, friend of the Muses. But as the archer-god, he is sudden death, as well as healing. He is the darkness as well as the clarity of prophecy. We shall visit two of his sanctuaries; both are in harsh mountain settings.

Today the visitor arrives at Delphi by a mountainous but modern road and walks comfortably from the car-park to the shrine. In ancient times she or he could have arrived by sea, landing at the nearby coast, or have travelled overland nearly 200 kilometres by the ancient road from Athens. Pausanias, a Greek-speaker and indefatigable traveller who lived in the Roman era in the second century AD, wrote a guide-book to Greece which is invaluable for understanding the Greek sites. He tells us, with a display of feeling unusual for him: '... the high-road ... to Delphi gets quite

9. Delphi: the theatre, temple, and panoramic view from the site.

precipitous and becomes rather difficult even for a fit man' (Pausanias 10.v.3). Despite the difficulty of the journey, Delphi was at least as attractive to visitors then as now. It held great significance throughout the Greek world and even beyond.

The main 'selling point' of the Delphic shrine was its oracle, the foremost oracle of the Greek world. In the temple sat the prophetess, the Pythia, who became ecstatic and prophesied as the mouthpiece of Apollo; priests then interpreted her messages. According to some ancient accounts, she descended into an oracular chamber, sat on a tripod, chewed

26

laurel leaves or just waited for the god. For years this process was recorded with scepticism. Recently, however, French geologists have identified a fault in the ground as a possible source of 'oracular' fumes, a mind-bending mixture of natural gases, and this fault was located precisely under the temple and the prophetic seat. Since antiquity, geological shifts in the rocks have closed off the source of inspiration. The discovery, if correct, explains the location of the shrine.

It will be seen from the plan (Fig. 10) that the sanctuary area was extremely crowded. The various features had to be carefully fitted into a limited space, and this was done over a long period of time. Buildings

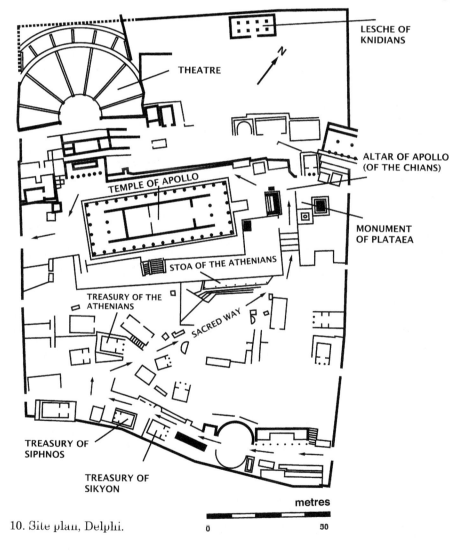

10. Site plan, Delphi.

accumulated, were destroyed and replaced in a kind of organic process. What is not apparent from the plan, and is hard to convey in a photograph, is the steep ascent. The Sacred Way makes two hair-pin bends, and the first two legs of the path are sharply ascending. As the close view is crowded with monuments and treasuries, it is clear that visitors are constantly confronted with something new and unexpected. At certain points they will be able to pause and appreciate a broad view of the mountain surroundings. But to take in the entirety of the site at once is impossible and so it appears much larger than it really is.

A distant view of the shrine suggests a few tiny buildings, huddled on a series of terraces in a cup of the mountain. However, when the visitor stands on the Sacred Way, surrounded by elaborate buildings and monuments, the skill of the planners is revealed. A 'sacred landscape' has been created on a human scale within the vast inhospitality of the mountain. This 'landscape' held potency throughout the Greek world for a thousand years.

In the prologue of Aeschylus' play, *Eumenides*, the Pythia stands outside the temple entrance praying; in her prayer, she makes reference to what she sees. Any previous visitor to Delphi – and there would have been many in the audience – would immediately recognise the famous view from the terraces. This is interesting as it suggests an appreciation of landscape not found in any surviving visual art, and alerts us that an ancient Greek would have been fully aware of the Delphic panorama. The priestess weaves into her speech mythical references to Apollo and his first coming to Delphi. She pictures him, sailing from Delos, his island birthplace, to the headlands of Attica, continuing in triumphal procession along the very same road that an Athenian visitor would have taken to Delphi and which is clearly visible from the temple platform. The Pythia's speech also reminds the audience of the archaic pediment sculpture in front of which the drama places her, for the entrance façade did indeed feature the arrival of Apollo by chariot, surrounded by a divine assembly. So, by means of sculpture and myth, the temple itself is seen as an interpreter of the place, its surroundings, and the experience of arriving there.

The Castalian Spring

The sacred Castalian Spring on the main road was a stopping-off point for worshippers, just before they reached the main sanctuary. The location of the spring is a wooded dell bounded by cliffs, which narrows at the back to a mysterious cleft in the mountain-side, possibly once the lair of Pytho. This spot is **numinous**, permanently twilit, because of the trees and the cliffs, a suitable spot for an encounter with the god. The sense of awe and mystery is reinforced by real danger as rocks can fall without warning from the cliffs.

The ritual importance of the spring is shown by two separate arrangements for approaching the spring-water. The more extensive one is Roman, demonstrating the continued popularity of the shrine in the period of Roman rule (*c.* second century BC onwards). The simpler archaic one (which would have been used in classical times) is right on the edge of the modern road. Water is channelled down from the wooded bank into a semi-subterranean masonry tank reached by stone steps. The ancient worshipper descended into the tank to reach the water, which is pure and chilly, fresh from the mountain. Here he or she was supposed to wash hands and hair in imitation of the god Apollo before entering the main sanctuary.

The Sacred Way

The modern visitor now enters the main sanctuary through the remains of the Roman **Agora**, just outside the original starting point of the visit. There is no monumental entrance or propylon to be seen, just an opening in the peribolos wall; but the Sacred Way is clearly defined as it rises steeply between walls and terracing on each side. The path will take the visitor through the whole site in three zig-zags or 'legs'.

Clustered around the entrance there were in classical times several major groups of life-size sculpture, arranged on raised stone platforms like little theatre stages. They were mainly victory monuments for wars between Greek city-states, but included the Marathon monument dedicated by Athens (after 490 BC), which featured a dozen impressive bronze figures by Pheidias: Athene, Apollo, the general Miltiades, Erechtheus, Cecrops – to name a few. One huge group commemorated Tegea's victory over Sparta, and another Sparta's victory over Athens. An unusual offering was the bronze Bull of Corfu, in thanks for an amazingly good catch of tunny fish. Pausanias' list of statues here is almost endless. After statue groups, a little higher up on the left, the visitor reaches treasuries.

The treasuries

Delphi was very rich in treasuries, tiny ornate buildings with a two-fold purpose. They were in themselves offerings to the god of the sanctuary and contained offerings. They were also show-cases for the cities which offered them: they formed a permanent presence for that city in the international centre and meeting-place which a Pan-Hellenic sanctuary was, and stood in permanent competition with the treasuries of other cities. These were all good reasons for a city to lavish the best it could of money, materials and craftsmanship on its treasury. At Delphi there were 30 or more treasuries whose foundations can still be seen; but many are unidentifiable. We shall look at two outstanding examples with substantial remains; one of them has been reconstructed.

11. Reconstruction drawing of the Siphnian Treasury, Delphi, *c.* 525 BC.

The Siphnian Treasury

The Siphnian Treasury (Fig. 11), an extremely sophisticated building in Ionic style, stood on the edge of the terracing to the left, on the first leg of the Sacred Way as the visitor faces uphill; it was raised on a high base of local limestone to bring its entrance up to the level of the path. Above the base it was impressively all marble, the first mainland building to be so. We know from Herodotus (*Histories* 3.57) that the islanders of Siphnos built it with a tithe of their profits from gold and silver mines at their time of greatest prosperity, and it was probably complete by 525 BC. Though, like all treasuries, it was small, it is easy to see how luxurious it was, and how totally it would put its neighbours in the shade. (Its fine fragments, now dismantled, are on show in the Delphi Museum.)

The building was designed, small though it is, to give delight to the viewer on all sides. Visitors would see the east side of the treasury (the back) as they approached, with sculpted pediment and frieze; they would then walk alongside the north frieze, which would not be too high up to admire in some detail. As visitors reached the west front of the building – which was spectacular – they could turn aside into a little paved forecourt, and there enjoy the famous view as well as a display of architectural

30

wonders: a super-elaborate façade with colourful maiden columns, a crowded little pediment and general air of sophisticated elegance.

Architectural detail

In plan, the treasury is a small temple-like rectangle with a single space inside, fronted by a **distyle in antis** porch. The two columns, however, are **caryatids** or statues of maidens (**korai**), standing on rectangular plinths and supporting the entablature and pediment on their cylindrical hats (**polos**) and tiny capitals. These delightful **korai** were once brightly decorated with paint, gilding and even little coloured glass gems, and actual jewellery. Piercings for their earrings can be seen in their ears. They stand in an upright columnar posture, pulling at their elaborate **chitons** (Ionic dresses) with one hand to reveal their figures – the fashionable pose for archaic girls. Even their polos hats and the capitals are carved with little scenes.

The Siphnian Treasury is enriched with unique narrative carving and with elaborate mouldings (Fig. 12), which articulate and emphasise every element of the architecture:

- The base of the exterior marble wall, just where it sits upon its limestone podium, has a colossal **bead-and-reel** moulding.
- The narrative frieze runs almost at the top of the exterior walls. Above is a small bead-and-reel under a larger 'tongue' or leaf border.
- The over-hang (soffit) of the roof is carved underneath with a bead-and-reel and a large lotus-and-palmette border (**anthemion**). Richness of decoration could hardly go further than this: the crispness of the carving alleviates the rich and heavy mix.

12. Drawing of mouldings from the Siphnian Treasury. *From top*: egg-and-dart, bead-and-reel, lotus-and-palmette (anthemion).

- The sima (gutter) was a double anthemion with lions' heads.
- The acroteria were probably sphinxes on the corners with central **nikai** (victory figures).
- The doorframe is wide and surrounded by extremely rich decoration; it acts as a dramatic frame for the **kore**-columns. Its uprights carry an anthemion with a small bead-and-reel; the lintel has a plain moulding with a band of spaced **rosettes** above; the lintel is supported at each corner by an inverted volute or scroll decoration.

The marble for the building was from Siphnos itself, the decorative borders are of Naxian and the sculpture is of Parian, the finest of **island marbles**. Although Parian marble itself was a luxury material, it was the transport of this heavy mass – undamaged – to the mountain site that was the main expense. Island sculptors probably accompanied it to execute the work with the required skill and understanding of the marble. This material was known to enable a finer finish on the carving than would limestone, but the planners set a new bench-mark for mainland opulence by using marble also for the whole building. Furthermore, they provided a full set of sculpture incorporating a continuous narrative frieze on all four sides, two tiny carved pediments and kore-columns, all bound together decoratively by the exquisite carved mouldings.

Pediments

Both pediments contained sculpture but only the scene from the east (the back) is preserved (Fig. 13). This pediment faced the ascending visitor and showed the rather odd but popular scene of Heracles attempting to steal the Delphic tripod from Apollo. A central taller figure, Zeus, adjudicates. What is successful in the composition is the axial central figure who is also the moral axis – with whom, clearly, the judgement rests. Yet across that central vertical, a violent struggle takes place, the diagonal lines of the tripod legs representing the to-and-fro of the argument. The struggle is thought-provoking – how can Heracles challenge the god Apollo in his own sanctuary? However, the viewer can rest assured that justice will prevail since Zeus is clearly in charge.

This miniature pedimental sculpture is carved in a somewhat experimental way that has never been copied; perhaps it was found to be a clumsy experiment. The lower half of each figure is carved in deep relief: the upper half is 'free-standing' in that the background slab has been cut deeply away.

Frieze

This sophisticated archaic work already shows the full range of tricks which frieze-designers can use for the ribbon format.

5. Delphi

13. The east pediment and east frieze of the Siphnian Treasury, Delphi, *c.* 525
BC. *Above*: Heracles attempts to steal the tripod of Apollo; *below left*: seated
gods; *below right*: scene from Trojan War.

Below the east pediment (Fig. 13), the viewer would also be rewarded
by a highly original stretch of frieze showing, to the left, seated gods in
animated conversation. The architectural nature of this carving is reflected in the repeated line of seats and in the flute-like folds of the
draperies. The originality of the design is to take social interaction as a
topic for narrative rather than battle or a procession. The talking gods are
then juxtaposed with a battle scene from the Trojan War, to the right,
thought to be the topic of the divine discussion. This parallelism worked
very well as narrative; but the asymmetrical arrangement was another
experiment which would not be repeated.
    Each side of the building has a different topic: the north frieze has an
especially strong narrative theme – the Battle of Gods and Giants (Fig. 14).
The story leads on from episode to episode, using various devices to link
the sections. As appropriate, Apollo and his twin sister Artemis are
central, while Themis, Athene, Aphrodite and other gods also form episodes,
overlapping to create depth and continuity. Fallen bodies make horizontal
links on the lower level, while glances and other interactions carry the eye
along the top level of the frieze. The north frieze is the side seen from the
Sacred Way: as the viewer walked on up, he would find gods steadily keeping
pace with him, while doomed giants head downhill (Fig. 11).

33

14. The north frieze of Siphnian Treasury, Delphi, *c.* 525 BC. *Below*: Gigantomachy: Themis in her chariot drawn by lions; giants; Apollo and Artemis (far right); *above*: leaf-and-dart moulding and small bead-and-reel.

The tiny building demonstrates what can be done with Ionic style, though making no use of the usual trademark volute capitals. The idea of the narrative frieze and sculpted pediments may in fact be a response to Doric decoration, since neither of these features is typical of Ionic in its homeland. Metopes from an earlier Delphic treasury, the Sikyonian, show very strong narrative which may have aroused a competitive response.

The Athenian Treasury

As visitors continued on up, rounding the first bend of the Sacred Way, they were next confronted with the Athenian Treasury (Fig. 15), which scores by its commanding position at the turning point. To those coming up, it presents a three-quarter angle, showing off both front and side-view, and for those descending, it gains in drama too.

The little triangular forecourt in front of the treasury may have been used to display war-trophies (possibly from Marathon); metal grilles once protected whatever was kept in the interior; one purpose of a treasury was to display prestigious loot.

The Athenian Treasury (6.6 x 9.7 metres) is a simple Doric cella with a distyle in antis porch, raised on a high platform without proper steps. The fine Doric frieze is sculpted (unusually) on all four sides; the tiny pediment also contained sculpture, and there were dramatic acroteria – horse-riding Amazons. Though the building is of conventional Doric design, the amount of sculpture and the material suggest conscious rivalry with the Siphnian masterpiece down the way. Of the three sorts of marble composing the

15. The Athenian treasury, Delphi, *c.* 500 BC.

Siphnian treasury, Parian was the finest, used only for the figurative sculpture. But the Athenian treasury extravagantly uses Parian throughout: this building is intended as an Athenian showpiece.

Frieze

The frieze, with its 30 metopes, contains two separate series that closely mirror each other. Each has a hero battling monsters, Heracles and Theseus – in many cases the same monster. Heracles was the hero par excellence of all the Greeks. Theseus, mythical king of Athens, was paradoxically credited with the founding of its democracy. (He was supposed to have introduced *synoikism* – the combining of the scattered villages of Attica into one cohesive city-state or polis. After doing this, he laid down his kingship in favour of the people (Plutarch, *Life of Theseus* 24).) As an unknown young man travelling to Athens from his birth-place Troizen, Theseus famously cleared the area of brigands such as Procrustes and Skiron. Arrived at Athens, he proved his identity to his father Aegeus, king of Athens. He soon went to Crete for his greatest exploit, the killing of the Minotaur; and his greatest shame – the abandoning of Ariadne. But on the treasury metopes he tackles a boar, a bull, an Amazon, all Heraclean exploits. Theseus is also seen standing in quiet companionship with Athene in the first and most conspicuous of the metopes.

The series showing Theseus was placed on the two prominent sides of the building, facing the ascending viewer. To see the Heracles metopes, one would have to leave the path and circle the building. While Heracles mirrors Theseus and adds sculptural richness, he is subordinated in position on this Athenian building while the 'democratic king' stands forth boldly.

Date

The second-century AD writer Pausanias believed that this treasury was built with spoils taken at the victory of Marathon in 490 (Pausanias 10.xi.4); some scholars accept a post-490 date, while others have suspected the building must be earlier because of the still-archaic sculptural style. There is also a suggestion that the treasury may commemorate an earlier event of significance equal to Marathon – and, in a way, closely connected – the foundation of the Athenian democracy in 507 BC. This date fits the sculptural style better; the idea could be corroborated by the subject matter of the metopes (though it would be equally appropriate for Marathon).

Parian marble may give another clue. While clearly this fine material could have been used at any time, by the period following Marathon the Athenians were beginning to develop their own marble quarries at Mount Pentelikon. This beautiful local stone was used for the great temple begun in Athens to celebrate Marathon after 490 and was usually the material of choice from that time on in Athens. But there was another Athenian building in Delphi already incorporating Parian marble – the entrance-front of the temple of Apollo, built by a prominent Athenian family, the Alkmaionids.

This aristocratic family was in exile at Delphi during the Peisistratid tyranny. They contracted to get the new temple built with funds that had been collected from many cities for the purpose. However, of their own free will, they paid more to replace limestone with Parian marble for the façade structure and its sculpture. This was clearly an astute move since from that time on, the grateful oracle constantly urged the Spartans to put a stop to the Peisistratid tyranny of Athens – and incidentally to the exile of their opponents, the Alkmaionids. By 510, the Spartans had helped the Athenians to expel the Peisistratids, and, as a result, a democracy was established in Athens. These events demonstrate the importance of 'the favour of Apollo', but also of the high value placed on buildings and the details of their construction.

The precedent of the Alkmaionid façade could for a short time have established Parian marble as – in a sense – a 'democratic', an Athenian and a 'fortunate' material, entirely appropriate for a treasury which might have acted as a thank-offering to Apollo and his favourable oracle for the new democracy.

The polygonal wall and the Athenian Stoa

Continuing up the Sacred Way on the second leg, a high, solid wall soon appears on the left (Fig. 16). This is the terrace wall, stabilising the huge artificial terrace essential for the very large temple of Apollo. It is built with **polygonal** blocks as an anti-earthquake measure. Though rather counter to the usual Greek aesthetic of clear angles and geometric form, there is much use of this polygonal feature at Delphi and it has clearly worked well. The joints still fit perfectly, but with random shapes which are planned not to slip apart as easily as rectangular blocks.

Along the same stretch of path, against the polygonal terrace wall, is the Athenian **Stoa**. This was a long, open, roofed platform, fronted by a colonnade of seven widely spaced slim Ionic monolithic columns. The wide spacing indicates a wooden superstructure, lighter than stone. This covered platform was intended to display spoils of war, including parts of captured ships. The Ionic style is explained by the fact that the naval victories celebrated were won jointly with Ionian allies.

The archaic Sphinx of the Naxians (565 BC), now in the museum, once

16. The Athenian stoa and polygonal terracing wall, Delphi.

17. The archaic Sphinx of the
Naxians on an Ionic capital,
Delphi Museum.

stood on its high Ionic column, just under the polygonal wall supporting
the temple terrace (Fig. 17). This victory monument is an outsize version
of a common type of archaic tomb decoration, suggesting a reference to the
war dead.

The visitor now walks the full length of the temple below the terrace
before rounding the next bend and climbing up steps to the level of the
temple forecourt. Opposite the temple entrance, another war memorial
with a more upbeat message was the triple bronze serpent surmounted by
a golden victory tripod, commemorating the important battle of Plataea
against the Persians. The names of the many allied Greek cities who fought
together were inscribed on the serpent's body, recording a rare inter-city
co-operation. (The remains of this triple serpent are now in Istanbul.)

As we have advanced along the Sacred Way, we have seen war celebrated in various ways. Inter-city conflict does not seem to have
embarrassed the Greeks much, and might seem almost like an extension
of athletic competition. Yet within the context of a Panhellenic shrine, all
Greeks must be thought of as meeting in neutral territory under the
influence of the god. This attitude is reflected in the enforced peace which

accompanied some religious festivals, notably the Olympic games and the Eleusinian mysteries. While the common enemy, Persia, can be proudly named and triumphed over, Greeks themselves should ultimately stick together, despite quarrels. What a shrine like Delphi or Olympia offers is one form of social cohesion, where, outside of any particular polis, common Greekness is celebrated.

The temple of Apollo

The visitor is now about to negotiate the steep steps leading to the temple forecourt. Pausanias gives a strange prehistory of the temple of Apollo:

> They say that the most ancient temple of Apollo was made of laurel, and that branches were brought from the laurel grove at Tempe. This temple would have been designed in the form of a hut. Next, the people of Delphi say the temple was made by bees out of beeswax and feathers ... as for the story about how they plaited a shrine out of feather-grass when it was still green, I shall not even start on it. The story that the third temple was made of bronze is no surprise ... the shrine of Athene of the Bronze House survives at Sparta to our times ... so a bronze temple for Apollo would not be unlikely (Pausanias 10.v.5).

This list may hint at pre-stone building methods. We get onto more secure ground with the archaic temple, burnt down in 548 BC. The temple of Apollo whose ruins can be seen today (Fig. 9) is the fourth-century temple built after the landslide of 373. But it preserves the layout and even the style of the late archaic temple completed by the Athenian Alkmaionids. This brief list indicates how many vicissitudes of accident (and perhaps fashion) a temple could go through. Delphi, being subject to earthquakes, was particularly vulnerable.

The building

At the entrance to the temple is a small forecourt bounded on one side by the temple steps and neat ramp and on the other by the altar of the Chians, clearly a prestigious offering which earned for its donor polis an important privilege: priority in consulting the oracle (*promanteia*). The enormous dark limestone rectangular block of the altar is made elegant by the addition of a creamy marble cornice on top and a similar moulding at its foot.

In this forecourt we may imagine the young hero Ion in Euripides' play of that name, sweeping the floor and scaring off the birds, in his role as temple servant (see Chapter 15); or the Pythia looking over the parapet at the view before entering the temple for her day's duty. Here we may imagine the queues of people wishing to consult the oracle (there is not much space), and a temple servant like Ion instructing them as to the procedure, checking their credentials and receiving their offerings.

Dark limestone makes up the platform steps and forecourt, creating a somewhat gloomy or awesome atmosphere. The style of the Doric columns visible today is massive, with the characteristic spreading archaic echinus; these columns may well be the archaic ones re-used. The **hexastyle** layout is still elongated in the archaic manner with fifteen columns down the flanks, but there is a practical reason for this. It is to accommodate an extra **adyton** or inner-chamber for the oracle. This fourth-century building seems to have copied its predecessor. There is now no visible trace of the oracular chamber in the foundations; though every visitor hopes to see it, it remains a mystery. The cella originally contained a stone called the Omphalos (navel) to mark the central point of the world. There was also a laurel tree, a statue of Apollo, and, oddly, the grave of Dionysus.

Prominent in the temple area was a famous feature: three inscriptions embodying Delphic wisdom. Two are well-known sayings: 'Nothing in excess' and 'Know thyself'. The third was totally cryptic even to the Greeks – a letter E.

The visitor can still walk all round the temple. On the downhill side, the dark limestone platform is built much higher as the ground falls away, and there is a gap here in the masonry for the exit of the sacred stream Cassiotis which once flowed right under the temple.

Architectural sculpture

The late archaic temple built by the Alkmaionids between 530 and 510 had a landmark marble front, as discussed above. Some of the archaic pediment sculptures can be seen in the museum. The entrance-front central motif seems to be the arrival of Apollo by chariot, with a frontal line-up of gods each side of him (Fig. 18). As can be seen, this method of representation results in a very small god. This disadvantage will be re-thought by subsequent pediment designers. At the corners of the composition are fantastic lions eating animal victims, so the bestial image of divine power is still represented (as seen on Corfu: Fig. 7), though a more humanist vision of deity is now taking centre place.

The back pediment probably featured a limestone battle between gods and giants. Athene, rushing in profile to her giant-slaying task,

18. Reconstruction drawing of the east pediment of the archaic temple of Apollo, Delphi, *c.* 515 BC.

and some fragments of giants can be seen in the museum. Zeus' chariot was possibly the centrepiece, paralleling Apollo's on the front pediment. However, this is mainly an action scene, executed in profile, whereas the front is confrontational.

The Lesche of the Knidians

Looking further up the slope (Fig. 10) between the temple and the cliffs, away from the main route, the ancient visitor would have seen the Lesche or club-house of the Knidians.

This was a simple stoa-like recreational building, decorated inside with very famous mural paintings by Polygnotos. The influence of this artist from the first half of the fifth century was felt throughout every form of Greek art. He introduced the idea of depicting contemplation rather than action. He also designed figures among landscape features, arranged up and down the full height of a wall rather than in the frieze-like arrangement familiar from pots or sculpture. Pausanias describes in great detail painted scenes from after the Fall of Troy, the Descent to the Underworld and other topics of a sad or thoughtful nature. The building was intended, according to Pausanias, for those who wanted to discuss 'old times and serious questions' (Pausanias 10.xxv.1). The paintings, with their moral challenges about war and justice, were certainly conducive to such talk.

The theatre, stadium and hippodrome

The last 'leg' of the path now zig-zags back on level ground, between the temple and the theatre. The theatre, being cupped in shape, is successfully accommodated to the terrain and is the only competition space within the temenos. The stone seating seen today was completed in the second century BC, monumentalising the earlier, less formal seating arrangement which took advantage of natural topography. There are 35 rows of seats with an audience capacity of 5,000. The first competitions held at Delphi were musical, Apollo being patron of music and art: sports were added later.

Continuing up from the theatre, visitors now leave the main temenos through a break in the peribolos wall, and ascend by a steep winding path through rocks and pine trees. They will be surprised to find a huge stadium 177.5 metres in length, fitted into a terraced area high above the sanctuary, round a shoulder of the mountain. Stone tiers of seating for 6,500 spectators are ranged on both sides of the track, and high stone piers mark the starting places for the runners. Before this stadium was made in the third century, footraces had been held down in the valley.

The famous bronze charioteer of Delphi (478/4 BC), damaged by earthquake, was found buried under the Sacred Way (Fig. 19): burial on-site was one way of dealing with spoiled offerings. Originally he formed only a

41

19. Bronze charioteer from Delphi, 478/4 BC.

part of a large statue-group of four beautiful bronze race-horses, a chariot and small groom. As he stood calmly on his chariot by the path between the theatre and the temple, his long fluted charioteer's dress must have taken on an architectural look, matching him deliberately with the adjacent Doric colonnade – two kinds of offering to the god. The dedicator of this showy expensive monument was Polyzalos, Tyrant of Gela in Sicily, reminding us how international the Greek world was and also that chariot-racing (as at Olympia) was the most spectacular and elite event at Delphi. The hippodrome for chariot-racing remained down on the valley floor at Crisa: this must have been a relief for the managers of the horses. The site is not identified.

5. Delphi

Athene Pronaia (Marmaria)

A second smaller sanctuary is found below the main road, between the spring and the sanctuary of Apollo. It too is steeply terraced, and contains several archaic and later temples including that of Athene Pronaia, treasuries (including that of Massilia – Marseilles) and other buildings, many unidentified.

The tholos

A **tholos** is the architectural star-turn of this sanctuary (Fig. 20), dated approximately 375 BC. It is a photogenic building, its pure white marble standing out dramatically against the backdrop of valley and mountain, as it must have been planned to do.

A tholos is circular – a shape used sparingly in Greek architecture, always attracting attention. A sense of mystery attaches to the circular plan, with associations of death, or the sacred hearth. The purpose of the tholos at Delphi is unknown, perhaps a shrine or treasury. Pausanias (who often seems rather visually unaware) does not note any round building in his description here. We know the architect – Theodorus of Phocaia – because Vitruvius records that he wrote a book about it, indicating that its design was of special interest.

20. Sanctuary of Athene Pronaia, Delphi: tholos, c. 475 BC.

Exterior

On a circular plinth (13.5 metres in diameter), an exterior Doric colonnade of 20 columns supported the normal Doric entablature. The columns are rather slimmer and placed closer together than they would be on a rectangular temple. This spacing avoids uncomfortable gaps on the profile of the building. The white marble cella wall is finished at the foot with a finely carved moulding of leaves, underlined by a strip of black limestone.

The metope frieze of the outer entablature was carved in deep relief. A smaller metope frieze in shallow relief circled the exterior cella wall, either below or above the roof of the colonnade. Examples from both sets are shown in the site museum.

A decorative gutter (sima) of foliage punctuated by lion-head water-spouts crowned the architrave and the metope frieze. On a rectangular temple, the sima enlivens the otherwise plain flanks: on a circular tholos, flank and façade are all one, giving extra emphasis to the entablature – which in a sense replaces the pediment.

The roof – a flattened cone – may have been in one unbroken section, or in two clear steps with the lower section roofing only the colonnade. As remnants of two simas have been found (one smaller than the other), either both sections of roof were edged with a decorative sima; or the higher sima demarcated the position of the cella wall, but without a step in the roof-line. The smaller scale of the higher sima would have given a sensitive perspective effect from below, (whatever the actual arrangement of the roofing). If the roof was stepped, there would have been a small vertical drum between the two levels; this could even have accommodated the smaller metope frieze and the smaller sima as a full second entabla-ture, using the existing elements in the most showy way possible. (Compare with the restoration of the Philippeion, an Ionic tholos at Olympia: Fig. 33.) A decorative acroterion crowned the apex: its practical purpose was to strengthen the central meeting point of the radiating roof beams. Eight radiating ridges with elaborate ridge-tiles supported upright palmettes, and perhaps small, coloured acroteria sculptures.

This unusually decorative roof would have been very clearly seen from above and at close quarters, since the main road between the two sanctu-aries runs just above the tholos where it stands on the lower terrace of Athene Pronaia.

Interior

Inside the cella was a ring-colonnade of ten columns, either half-columns, or full columns just touching the wall in order to maximise the central space. Their placement corresponded to every alternate column of the outer ring, and they stood raised on a limestone bench running all round the wall: this made them shorter, more slender and space-saving. The

44

capitals were Corinthian, like those at Bassae (see Fig. 76). The use of a decorative new style, Corinthian, is thus confirmed as an interior feature in Greek architecture.

The building was of white marble, but used black limestone for colour contrast. The decorative strip circling the base of the exterior cella walls was black, as was the interior bench. The paving of the cella floor was black with a white disk in the centre. These colour effects would have served to emphasise the circularity of the form.

The gymnasium

Adjacent to this sanctuary area were a gymnasium and other sports facilities, on more terraces. On an upper level was a long covered track (**xystos**) for bad-weather training. Directly below were the **palaistra** with a peristyle court and separate rooms opening off two sides of it. Next to that was a circular plunge pool. This was fed with cold mountain water, which ran into basins from bronze lion-head spouts fixed in the terrace wall, and then flowed into the pool. Later the Romans added a heated bath complex.

Votive offerings and monuments at Delphi

Though the Sacred Way still guides the visitor through the temenos upwards to the temple and beyond, what is now missing from a visit to Delphi, as with any ancient sanctuary today, is the proliferation of votive offerings, statues and monuments of all sorts. (A few have been mentioned.) Those dedicated by individuals mostly commemorated athletic victories, but state dedications were predominantly monuments to military victories. Treasuries could also be thank-offerings for victories – implying an influx of funds – ten per cent was expected by the god. Treasuries or major war monuments could be placed defiantly opposite your defeated enemies' monument, especially when that former victory was over you! In the crowded conditions at Delphi, this kind of juxtaposition was common.

Other dedications can be seen in the museum in a variety of types and materials: archaic **chryselephantine** gods, exquisite ivory miniatures, down to the humble moulded terracotta votive offerings. The life-size archaic silver bull, with its golden mane and hooves must once have been an amazing sight; still impressive today, in its glass case, though squashed and pieced together.

'Cleobis and Biton' are twin archaic **kouroi** dating from c. 580 BC. They are chunky youths with archaic smiles, archaic clenched fists, unusual little boots, and a certain naïve radiance in their broad faces. A story attaches to them, told by Herodotus (*Histories* 1.31). Cleobis and Biton were sons of a priestess of Argive Hera. When she lacked transport for the journey to the temple, her sons took the place of oxen, yoking themselves to her chariot. The grateful mother prayed for the greatest blessing of all for these devoted sons: they died in their sleep then and there. Though the story fits the statues nicely, they might have been originally intended as Castor and Pollux, the heavenly twins, commonly worshipped together: however, that is not such an exciting story for a guide to tell.

These few statues, randomly preserved from the multitudes once crowding the sanctuary, give an idea of the variety and richness of offerings, and the great interest they added to a visit to the complete site.

Conclusion

Delphi, home of the oracle, includes the experience of the whole landscape: the twin peaks of Parnassos, the Castalian spring in its rocky gorge, the mingled sun and storm of the valley, Marmaria (the lower sanctuary), and the Corycian cave of the nymphs high on the untracked mountain. When Dionysus took over the shrine for the winter session, Bacchants roamed far and wide under the influence of the god – Bacchants who were normally you and your neighbours.

Sophocles, poetically contemplating the source of the divine word, imagines it as emanating not from the Pythia herself but from all of the various elements of the place: 'Rock-face of Delphi speaking the word of god … manifest voice ringing clear from snow-bound Parnassos … power of prophecy from the central heart of earth' (Sophocles, *Oedipus the King* 462-81).

Despite suspicions of collaboration with the Persian enemy and the occasional evidence of bribery, the shrine and oracle of Delphi held immense prestige in the Greek world for over a thousand years. The last oracle is recorded as an epitaph for a great institution: the young pagan emperor Julian in the fourth century AD, who tried to fight Christianity and revive the old religion, received this answer to his inquiry about the state of the shrine:

> Go tell the king, the well-wrought house is fallen
> No shrine has Phoebus now, no prophetic laurel,
> No speaking spring; quenched is the chattering water.
> Cedrenus, cited in *Works of the Emperor Julian*,
> Loeb edn, vol. III, p. lvii

6

Olympia

The Olympic games traditionally date from 776 BC. The ancient Greeks used this year as the start of their dating system, indicating the importance of the games. The cult of Zeus is thought to have been established on the site as early as the tenth century, developing by gradual stages into a Panhellenic athletic festival.

The site of Olympia is unusual for Greece – as different as possible from Delphi – open and flat, green and lush, low-lying between slow, strong rivers and mounded, wooded hills. Today there are vivid blossoming trees and wildflowers, meadow-like grass, a tranquil atmosphere. The air is soft and pleasant, the view of the sky vast. There is no formal planning, no axial line-up, but a relaxed, spacious layout of the various amenities.

In antiquity, the sanctuary was a great deal fuller than it is today, since statues, altars and monuments crowded wherever they could find a free spot; and complete buildings take up more visual space than do ruins. But still, the open sky and the low hills would have ensured the same spacious feeling. Zeus, king of gods and sky-god, was usually worshipped in broad level open sites like this one.

Though located apparently in the middle of nowhere, the sanctuary was really very accessible for visitors, as its ancient success proves. Olympia is about 30 kilometres from the coast and lies in a rolling landscape of shallow valleys. Two rivers, Alphaios and its tributary Kladeos, border the site – and on occasion flood it, increasing its fertility. On the north boundary is a richly wooded sacred hill, Kronion, or the Hill of Kronos (Zeus' father).

The central sacred area or temenos of Olympia was known as the Altis (this word is a version of *alsos*, Greek for 'grove'). The sanctuary still has the character of a grove, with wild olive, oaks, pines, planes and poplars; Pausanias mentions the plane trees of the Altis, the poplars for firewood and the wild olive for garlands. In the earliest days when the sacred Altis was just a natural grove, worshippers probably hung their offerings from the branches of trees. The developed Altis contained the main altar of Zeus, two main temples, two hero shrines, and a large variety of other dedications. At some time, a wall was built enclosing the Altis and marking it off from the outer area (Fig. 21).

Surrounding the Altis were other permanent features vital to the running of the sanctuary and the festivals: to east and west, sports facilities, to north and south, administrative buildings. Beyond this built-

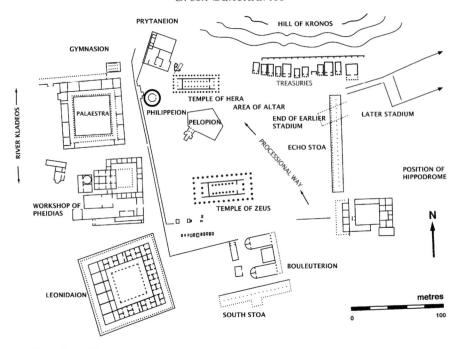

PRYTANEION

HILL OF KRONOS

GYMNASION

TREASURIES

TEMPLE OF HERA

AREA OF ALTAR

PALAESTRA

PHILIPPEION

PELOPION

END OF EARLIER STADIUM

LATER STADIUM

RIVER KLADEOS

ECHO STOA

PROCESSIONAL WAY

POSITION OF HIPPODROME

TEMPLE OF ZEUS

WORKSHOP OF PHEIDIAS

BOULEUTERION

N

LEONIDAION

metres

SOUTH STOA

0   100

21. Site plan, Olympia.

up area was plenty of open space for the temporary necessities of the festival: care of horses, stabling and pasture, visitor campsites, food outlets, water-sellers and so on.

The games took place every four years in August. There was a guest-house for the select few, but mainly the visitors had to camp. The balmy climate of Olympia must at that season have been oppressively hot and humid – harsh for the athletes – but campers were probably assured of acceptable sleeping conditions. Camping at Olympia is sometimes said to have been unpleasant, particularly because good drinking water was in short supply. For those who disliked the outdoor life, there would be compensation for discomfort in the sight of superb naked athletes and the drama of high-level competition. But not every camper was uncomfortable, and competition was not only on the race-course. The assembling of Greeks from every level of society and from all over the Greek world offered an important opportunity for social display. Plutarch gives the example of two young and politically ambitious Athenians competing as campers: 'When [Themistocles] went to Olympia ... he tried to rival Cimon in the dinners he gave and in the magnificence of his furniture and the tents in which he entertained his visitors' (Plutarch, *Life of Themistocles* 5). Clearly camping at Olympia could reach very high standards indeed. Many rich men would be present, competing especially in chariot events;

their entourage and equipment would be expected to add to the glittering spectacle.

The Olympic games were the oldest and foremost of the main four on the athletic circuit – Olympic, Pythian (Delphi), Nemean, Isthmian. A well-off young man of the sixth or fifth century might do the circuit of all four games and devote much leisure to training seriously. Euripides makes his mythical character Hippolytus say anachronistically: 'I would wish to come first in the Pan-Hellenic competitions, and to be second in politics ...' (Euripides, *Hippolytus* 1016-19). Hippolytus is the illegitimate son of King Theseus and can never be king; he tailors his ambitions to those of a private gentleman who would bring honour to his city if he were successful, and would receive honour in return – in the form of statues, poems, free dinners and probably cash. The celebrity acquired by an athlete could also be used to gain advancement in politics: for example, an Athenian, Cylon, attempted a political coup in the late seventh century on the strength of his Olympic victory (Herodotus, *Histories* 5.70). Alcibiades, a well-born Athenian 'celebrity' figure of the later fifth century, made an enormous impression with seven teams of racing chariots at Olympia, scooping up at least three top wins. For this, he was acclaimed and wooed by other cities with rich gifts, including a 'magnificently decorated tent' and food and wine to enable the lavish entertainment clearly expected of a man in his position at the games (Plutarch, *Life of Alcibiades* 12). Understandably, the role of athlete changed and became increasingly professionalised in later centuries.

Manning a sanctuary

Modern Olympia serves just one purpose – tourism. In ancient days it must have been much the same, since the sanctuary served no one community but the whole of the Greek world. Obviously the activity intensified greatly for the four-yearly festival, but the sanctuary was running all the time. For example, Pausanias on his visit tells of sacred guides who show him the sights and explain them. In addition to the governing committee, a huge staff would have been necessary at all levels to manage such a major shrine on a daily basis: officials to deal with distinguished visitors, staff for crowd control, priests and lesser acolytes to see to all the practical details of the sacrifices, groundsmen to keep up the sports facilities, medical attendants – especially for sports injuries, masseurs and bathing attendants, caretakers to maintain the whole site. For the festival, valuable horses would have to be accommodated, would need to be fed and cared for over some days, even weeks, might have to be recuperated from a sea-voyage or long journey. Pausanias tells us there were woodsmen who cut poplar wood especially for the sacred fire of sacrifices (3.xiii.3), and others who had the hereditary task of caring for the great gold-and-ivory statue of Zeus:

Pheidias's descendants, who are called the polishers and who were granted
by Elis the office of cleaning dust and dirt from Zeus' statue, offer sacrifice
at the altar of Athene ... the Worker, before they begin their polishing
(Pausanias 5.xiv.5).

There were over 60 altars, not associated with temples. Pausanias tire-
lessly lists them all – 'in the same order in which the Eleans sacrificed'
which they did 'once a month'. These sacrifices were 'in antique style ...
they burn frankincense with honey cakes on the altars, and lay olive-
branches on them and pour wine.' They were staffed by a 'priest (elected
for the month), prophets, and wine-carriers, a sacred guide and a flute-
player and the woodman' (who would have supplied wood and lit the fires)
(Pausanias 5.xv.10). These details give an idea of the ceaseless religious
activity which would have gone on in a major shrine.

As the shrine grew more complex in later years, with its hotel, the
Leonidaion, built in the fourth century, and, much later, the club-house
built by the Emperor Nero, there would have been more and more staff
required. Altogether, Olympia was a going concern for more than a thousand years, constantly changing and growing, and always successful.

Control of the sanctuary

The site was managed by Elis, a small polis situated some 30 kilometres
away. This city, not particularly distinguished in other ways, had the
major role in running the site for most of its history. Another city, Pisa,
closer to Olympia, historically vied with Elis for control of the shrine, since
it was a source of enormous income as well as prestige. In 471 BC Elis
finally wiped Pisa off the map – its site is not even known – and won
uncontested control of the sanctuary. According to Pausanias, the funds
for building the temple of Zeus came from the profits of this war between
Elis and Pisa.

Olympia flourished after the Persian wars. A major Panhellenic sanctuary, Olympia was remote from that theatre of war and was particularly
accessible to the west. Elis was not implicated in any politics yet did send
a small force to fight. In contrast, Delphi, somewhat more accessible to the
east, a shrine of equal or greater fame (because of its oracle), had not been
seen as supportive to the Greek cause, and was suspected of inclining too
much towards Persia. Olympia seized the double advantage of increased
funding and a clean political reputation to honour Zeus with a new temple.

The Sacred Way

A Sacred Way should lead worshippers from the entrance to the altar. At
Olympia, the sacred way seems to be just a natural route between monuments. Pausanias refers to the processional entrance, but as this could be

a Roman addition, it might even be that the entrance and the sacred route have been changed over the years; no route is now clearly demarcated. In this respect Olympia is a complete contrast to Delphi where the Sacred Way is almost sculpted into the landscape, and with its three 'legs' is clearly defined by the buildings lining its steep ascent.

The temple of Hera

Of the two large temples at Olympia, the oldest is an early archaic building, *c.* 600-580, dedicated to Hera. In a sanctuary of Zeus, this is a little puzzling, though it is a reminder that the temple was not the most vital element in worship: the altar was. Worship of Zeus was centred on his open-air 'ash altar' (described below) and continued to be so after his fine new temple was built.

Pausanias tells us that the cult statues he saw were an enthroned Hera and, next to her, a standing Zeus with beard and helmet (Pausanias 5.xvii.1). A stone head of Hera can be seen in the museum, an archaic piece of about the same date as the temple; it may be that the vanished body was of wood. It has been suggested that this temple was really Zeus' before the classical one was built.

The building

The temple of Hera is interesting because, though currently dated at about 580 BC, it was built in an already outdated seventh-century way, using mud-brick for the walls on a base of stone, and a superstructure of wood with a roof of terracotta tiles and a wooden colonnade. Still visible today (Fig. 22) is the limestone platform with two steps only and neat masonry of the cella to a height of one metre, upon which the perishable materials were constructed.

The proportions are archaic. The front was hexastyle but the sides were elongated with sixteen columns; these were widely spaced too, which indicates a lighter architrave of wood rather than stone. However, already the corner columns were more closely placed than the others – this variation could suggest a Doric triglyph/metope frieze above, as contraction of column spacing solved a design problem at the corners (see p. 87).

The few standing stone columns (some monolithic) are a non-matching set in a stocky Doric style. We know from Pausanias that they were added one by one, over time, by different donor cities, to replace the original wooden ones, the first stone addition being not long after the building of the temple. When Pausanias wrote his book in 173 AD, just one wooden column still remained – in the back porch. The fact that each city made no attempt to match their offering to the rest suggests that there was a desire for the individual offering to be seen as such. This idea is reinforced by the fact that some columns are cut to receive a dedication tablet.

22. Temple of Hera, Olympia, *c.* 580 BC.

This antiquity of construction seems strange for a major temple in a major sanctuary. Very many temples were accidentally destroyed and, in the process of replacement, were also updated. It may be that the temple of Hera, though a bit outdated even when first built, acquired, as time passed, a special sacredness of nostalgia. It was 750 years old when Pausanias observed its single wooden column – a venerable column that would have 'seen so much'!

In the Olympia museum are the remnants of a vertical terracotta disk two metres across, heavily patterned with concentric geometric borders. This was the pedimental decoration or acroterion of the Heraion: there would have been one at each end of the temple. Similar patterned disks (though not so large) have been found in sanctuaries near Sparta – suggesting that this is a specially Peloponnesian design feature.

Inside the cella was an unusual arrangement. In order to avoid putting too much stress on the mud-brick cella walls, the outside columns were lined up with those of the interior colonnade, the object being for two sets of columns to carry each of the beams that supported the inner ceiling and heavy tile roof. Originally, each alternate interior column was attached to the cella wall by a little 'spur wall' creating a series of alcoves.

Contents

The temple of Hera eventually became something of a museum for precious artworks. While the cult statues of Hera and Zeus were early archaic, or as Pausanias puts it: 'simple-minded', there were many more sophisticated sculptures and objects of gold and ivory on display. The marble Hermes of Praxiteles (possibly an ancient copy) now in the museum was excavated from one of the alcoves; and there was also the famous archaic chest of Kypselos, decorated with a whole compendium of myths – described at great length by Pausanias, who loves a story. The first scene was the chariot race of Oinomaus and Pelops: the foundation myth of Olympia. Pelops was seen racing in his chariot with his bride-to-be, Hippodameia, and their chariot-horses were growing wings, so they are supernatural. This is a story we will meet again.

The temple of Zeus: 471-457 BC

By the second quarter of the fifth century it must have become evident that an archaic mud-brick temple, an ash altar and an earth stadium in a natural hollow of the ground were hardly impressive, no matter how prestigious the games or the festival. With increased funds from the conquest of Pisa, the Eleans could enhance their acquisition appropriately. The building of the temple of Zeus thus fitted the needs of the Elean managers of Olympia at this time, and must also have chimed with the general triumphal mood of Greece as a whole after the defeat of Persia. Although the struggle was not completely over, mainland Greece seemed secure, thanks to the co-operative effort of most of the city-states and its distance from the war zones. The final stages of the war took place either by sea or on the eastern borders of the Mediterranean. With funding and security at Olympia, the way was now clear to build a temple suitable for the king of the gods in his major sanctuary. In particular, this temple would need to surpass that of Delphi.

The building

The new temple was clearly planned as the monumental centre of a prestigious shrine (Fig. 23). It is situated almost parallel to that of Hera (Fig. 21), at a comfortable distance so that both temples roughly face the important ash altar, as well as the rising sun. There were no factors to limit the design and it seems few restraints on expense. The temple of Zeus is enormous (27.68 x 64.12 metres) and its size still impresses today, even now that all the columns are felled and, except for the high platform, scarcely one stone remains on another. Zeus, sky-god, is huge and one certainly feels it, looking even at the ruins of his house.

The temple is of course Doric, the mainland style. Sometimes it is called the 'classic' Doric temple – or even, disparagingly, the 'bog standard' Doric temple. The temple is – as Pausanias puts it – built of 'local stone' and designed by a 'local man' called Libon. Despite criticisms of its 'dullness', it should be seen as superbly fitting for its purpose: to impress, to provide an up-to-date architectural focal point for a major sanctuary, to express the character of Zeus, king of the gods.

23. Reconstruction view of Olympia showing the temple of Zeus and the earth altar, by Friedrich Adler from Ernst Curtius & Friedrich Adler, *Olympia*, vol. 2 (Berlin, 1896).

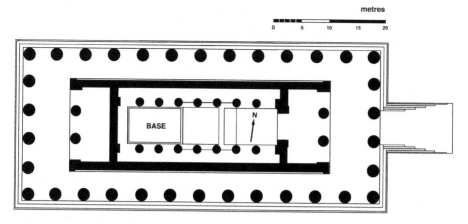

24. Ground plan, temple of Zeus, Olympia, 470-458/7 BC.

If the temple of Zeus is standard Doric, it may be because in fact it sets the standard (Fig. 24). Its 'formula' of 6 columns to the front and 6 x 2 + 1 to the flanks results in a pleasing classical proportion. A glance back at the elongated late-archaic temple at Delphi will show that this classical layout seems up-to-date and smart in comparison.

The proportions of the new temple were carefully worked out to form a rational system of relationships: for example, the distance between each column centre and the next was half the height of a column. A similarly proportionate system has made the Parthenon famous as a model of Greek rationality and harmony. The collapsed state of the temple of Zeus makes it impossible now to detect this virtue of proportion, yet if the building were complete the eye would perceive it unconsciously and be pleased.

The temple is set upon the usual three-stepped platform: the format of a Doric temple remains the same, whatever the size. Because of the resulting great height of each step, a ramp is inserted leading up to the entrance on the east. The platform is built of the same local limestone as the rest, and is fairly intact to this day. Its immense, close-fitting blocks have survived disastrous earthquakes which toppled everything else.

The 'local material' used is **shelly limestone**, a coarse-grained stone which cannot take very fine detail and weathers poorly. When the temple was complete, the rather rough shelly surface would have been finished off with marble-dust **stucco**, making a smooth marble-like protective surface. The whole building was constructed of this stone, except for the gutters, lion-head waterspouts, roof-tiles and sculptures – all these were of imported Parian marble.

The architrave, frieze and pediments were classical Doric (Fig. 25). The column capitals have the compact, neat mid-fifth-century profile, very different from those of the temple of Hera, which are mainly in the

25. Reconstruction of the east front, temple of Zeus, Olympia.

spreading archaic style. The sturdy column shafts contributed to the massive effect of the building; and they themselves were massive enough to visually support an entablature of heavy proportions. The outer metopes were plain; the pediments were furnished with particularly spectacular sculpture. The central acroteria were gilded bronze Victories, the outer ones were gilded bronze tripods: tripods were athletic prizes in Homer, so military and athletic victory is teamed on the roof decoration.

The spacing of the corner columns of the outer colonnade was slightly reduced (see p. 87). The porches and the corridor (**pteroma**) of the outer colonnade were particularly spacious and would have provided a promenade area. The porches were distyle in antis, the back porch (opisthodomos) being a dummy, purely for symmetry, but providing a pleasant, shady, elevated area for the visitor (Fig. 24).

It was this prominently placed back-porch, facing towards the palaistra, which Herodotus picked as the perfect platform for a public reading from his new book: *The Histories*. Here, the unknown visitor from Halicarnassus was able to attract enough attention to establish his immediate fame as a Greek writer, demonstrating what a lively, alert crowd attended the games.

Within both porches there was a surprise, since the inner metopes were sculpted (Fig. 26).

56

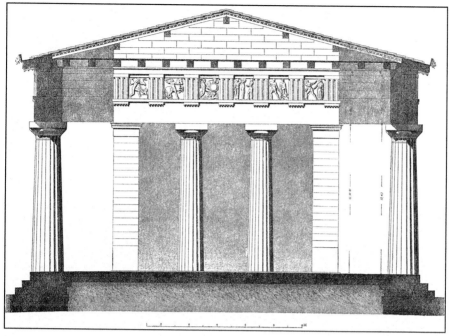

26. Reconstruction of the inner porch, temple of Zeus, Olympia, showing the metopes.

The cella and the statue of Zeus

All this exterior spaciousness left a comparatively small cella (Fig. 27). It had a central 'nave' divided from the side 'aisles' by two colonnades, each of seven small-scale double-decker columns separated by an entablature. This two-storey arrangement enables an economical use of space, as the columns can be slimmer.

It is not known whether there was a statue originally – possibly the archaic standing Zeus was brought over from the temple of Hera. In any case, at some time following 432 BC, some 20 years after the completion of the temple, the interior was slightly adapted to accommodate a colossal new statue of Zeus. Either originally or at that time, the upper storey of each double colonnade was made to carry a viewing gallery which could be reached by a winding wooden stair inserted each side of the entrance.

The enthroned Zeus was about twelve metres high, and his implied size was greater: if he ever stood up he would raise the roof. He was crowned with wild olive, like Olympic victors. His flesh was ivory while the large expanse of his golden robe was 'wrought with animals and lily-flowers'. In one hand was a Victory, a sizeable statue in itself, and in the other a sceptre, 'flowering' with precious metals and topped with Zeus' eagle.

27. Cross-section of the temple of Zeus, Olympia, showing the colossal statue of Zeus.

Every part of the throne was adorned with mythical characters and beasts, while the gold finish was varied with ebony, ivory and coloured gems. The god himself appeared to be made of solid gold and ivory, though in fact these materials were a veneer pieced together on a core of carved wood. This use of gold and ivory (chryselephantine) was an ancient technique whose other-worldly effect was perfect for representing divinity.

Pheidias, designer of the statue, must have felt that the massiveness and comparative plainness of the temple were an appropriate foil for this daring project. How easily the ornate colossus could have become ridiculous – but instead it was judged 'to add something to established religion, so closely did the majesty of the work match the deity himself' (Quintilian, *Institutio Oratoria* 12.10.7-9). This majestic Zeus could truly be seen as the king of heaven, moving away from the naughty Zeus of myth to embody ideas of power and justice.

The statue-plinth is known from Pausanias to have been black **Eleusinian limestone**, and it can still be seen today in the ruins, taking up the entire width between the two 'nave' colonnades. In front of the statue, Pheidias had an innovative feature inserted, also still visible: a large shallow pool, also of black limestone and with a raised rim of white

Pentelic marble. Since the pool was as wide as the plinth, an adjustment had to be made to fit the pool rim to the column feet (a clue that Pheidias' input was something of an afterthought to the original design). The dark pool was filled with olive oil. Pausanias tells us that the oil was to counteract the humid atmosphere's effect on the statue, half of ivory on a basis of wood – two organic and unstable materials. Probably the hereditary 'polishers' used the oil on the statue to stabilise it, and perhaps poured it into the wooden core as well. Whatever the practicalities, the aesthetic effect of the pool would have been great. Any filtered sunlight or lamplight would have created a vast mysterious mirror of oily darkness in which the glittering gold and glimmering ivory would be reflected in calm or in movement.

The plinth and the pool together took up two-thirds of the space within the 'nave'. This was acceptable, since the main purpose of any temple was to house the statue. (Even if there was – as sometimes – no statue, a temple was still by implication the house of the god.) The space was further limited by fencing in the central nave with decorated low screens between the columns, both to the front and the sides. This cut down access to the precious statue, but serious tourists could probably get nearer to it via the side-aisles and also get a good view from the gallery, as Pausanias did. From his detailed description it is clear that a close view repaid the effort.

On the black stone plinth of the statue, another scene was worked in attached gold or gilded figures. This represented the birth of Aphrodite from the sea, with many attendant gods to welcome her; the divine assembly was framed at each end by the rising chariot of the Sun, the sinking steed of the Moon.

Pheidias' workshop and the statue of Zeus

Just outside the temenos area (Fig. 21), to the south-west of the temple, Pheidias' workshop can still be seen, at least the lower courses of its walls. Many terracotta moulds were excavated here in which the folds of the golden robe of Zeus were formed and also moulds to make coloured glass 'gems'. With them was another treasured evidence of Pheidias' presence – a plain black mug with the rough inscription: 'I belong to Pheidias'. These items, now in the museum, identify the building.

The interesting thing about this workshop is that it reproduces the dimensions of the nave area where the Zeus was to be placed. The inference is that the statue was planned precisely for its available space: height, width and depth – possibly even the same lighting might have been reproduced in the workshop. The sculptor had exactly calculated the overwhelming effect of the enormous enthroned god in his temple. As a matter of fact, such sculpture workshops were probably routine on sanctuary construction sites. But since the Zeus of Olympia has often been criticised for its 'overcrowded' proportions within the cella, this workshop offers a specific answer to the criticism.

Pausanias finishes his description of the Zeus with this rather naive tribute:

> I know the recorded dimensions of height and width of the Zeus at Olympia, but I shall not recommend those who measured them since the dimensions claimed by them fall a long way short of the impression this statue has created in those who see it ... (Pausanias 5.xi.9).

Pausanias is no art critic – or he could have added that it was the careful calculations of the designer, Pheidias, which created this deliberate effect of size. Instead he tells us that Zeus himself commended the work with a thunderbolt, in answer to Pheidias' prayer.

The statue was eventually taken to Constantinople where it may have influenced the representation of Christ in the development of Byzantine Christian art; it was accidentally destroyed by fire in the fifth century AD. It has left a few material traces of its existence: the finds from the workshop of Pheidias displayed in the museum, the black limestone base and black pool floor, still to be seen in the denuded cella. Coins give an idea of the face and general design of Zeus.

Architectural sculpture

Like the gold and ivory statue of Zeus, the pedimental sculpture of the temple of Zeus represents a major financial investment. Reducing the enterprise to these crude terms, we should enquire what goals would justify all this expense. The new temple of Zeus, by its location, quality and size was making a declaration of significance which would reflect upon the whole sanctuary, the games, and their precedence in the Pan-Hellenic festival world. Delphi, second on the list, already had its large-size oracular temple with impressive pediments. The temple of Apollo at Delphi must have been a competitive inspiration to the Olympic managers. The temple at Delphi had contrasting pediments: a frontal line-up of divine persons (bracketed by beasts) and probably a fight-scene – a Gigantomachy. Turning to the new Olympic pediments, we find a similar pattern, but an even more impressive presentation.

The east pediment

The east pediment features a frontal line-up, surrounding the god of the temple (Fig. 25). The plain and solemn 'severe style' of the carving fits the heavy Doric architecture perfectly. All five central figures are as straight as the columns above which they stand, and even the fluting of the columns is echoed in the folds of the women's long dresses. This relationship with the building can now only be seen in a reconstruction: the actual sculptures are in the Olympia Museum.

There are several improvements on the Delphic scheme, helped by the move from late archaic to early classical style. The archaic beasts have been dropped in favour of a unified theme. The central god, Zeus, is not smaller – as was made inevitable by the chariot of Apollo – but is appropriately larger than all other characters and fits well in the apex: this may have an important psychological effect on the viewer, as we shall see. The supporting cast are not just standing frontally as separate statues, but are now a dramatic group, with psychological awareness of each other, bound together in an intense retelling of the myth. Each figure is not just characterised as young, old, male female, etc., but also interprets its own part in the story with appropriate body-language. The viewer at Olympia is not just confronted, but is also drawn in; by being encouraged to puzzle out the meaning of each figure, he or she is challenged to interpret and to respond for himself – or herself, since this story is not only of a victory but also of a marriage. Zeus is present as the one who judges – but it is left to the viewer to contemplate the judgement.

The subject of the sculpture on the east pediment is 'the preparation for the chariot race between Pelops and Oinomaos' as Pausanias usefully tells us. The story of Pelops' chariot-race is also the story of how he won his bride, Hippodameia. She was a princess whose wicked father, Oinomaos, was king of Pisa. He was reluctant to let her marry, and any suitor of hers had to win her in a chariot-race against him; the penalty for losing was immediate death. Already thirteen suitors were decorating Pisa with their severed heads when Pelops arrived. This time Hippodameia fell in love. From here, the story has several versions. The nice version is the one we have seen on the chest of Kypselos – Pelops had magic winged horses given to him by Poseidon. Other versions involve the bribery of Oinomaos' charioteer Myrtilos, sabotage of his master's chariot's lynchpins by replacing them with wax, and, finally, destruction of the complicit charioteer, who managed to curse the house of Pelops before he died.

Mythology is a rag-bag from which artists can pick the version that suits their purpose best. Cheating was utterly forbidden at the games and some argue that the pediment represents a warning to athletes not to cheat; but, vital as this issue was, it would make a poor theme for the most important sculpted area in the sanctuary. What we actually see is the king of the gods amid the preparation for a race on which a great deal will hang – the life and fame of Pelops, the fate of Hippodameia whose father is wronging her by preventing her marriage. As spectators, we can only hope that the best man will win – as in any athletic competition – and he will, if the gods favour him. Zeus, god of Justice, is thought (although his head is missing) to incline towards Pelops whom we may trust is the chosen and destined winner.

61

The figure of Oinomaos, hand on hip, looks overconfident as he explains the cruel terms of the race. His wife, Sterope, looks worn out, and holds her hands in a grieving or thoughtful posture. Hippodameia stands at the ready because she will ride in the chariot with Pelops. She hints at her wishes by lifting part of her veil, a recognised gesture indicating willingness for marriage.

This story was the foundation myth of Olympia; Pelops, the winner, gave his name to the Peloponnese and was the founder of the Olympic games.

More sanctuary themes are found further along the pediment. The famous rivers, probably the first ancestors of all other river-god statues, are lying in the extremities of the triangular field, where diminishing figures are needed. They are characterised as slow-flowing Alpheios on the left and its livelier tributary, Kladeus, on the right. Another geographical reference may be the young boy crouching: he is sometimes identified as Arcas, the boy-hero of neighbouring Arcadia.

Last but not least are the two groups of horses. Animals are popular on pediments because they bring a desirable variety of organic form, especially useful for creating horizontals and carrying the eye pleasantly along the pediment slope. The four-horse teams introduce a note of physical power: horses were the sports cars of antiquity. Here the viewer will look up into the mass of legs and appreciate the display of fine horse-flesh, seen unusually from below. The promise of power and speed varies the stillness of the composition as a whole; in fact this chariot race will be a kind of metaphor for the human catastrophe to come, but also for the daring and achievement of the victor. Horses are very relevant to the Olympic setting, and these face the hippodrome area.

The role of sculpture

The mere presence of sculpture, but especially if of impressive quality, was a political claim to importance. Sculpture on a temple was capable of pulling together messages, not only about the building, but also relating to the whole sanctuary. We shall see that the temple of Zeus sculptural programme interprets the sanctuary as a whole.

Taking the sanctuary on its simplest level, as a venue for athletic competition, there is reference in the sculpture to many of the competitions: chariot racing on the front, wrestling on the back, and, in the metopes, many forms and approaches to competition. These references spin out to the various sports locations of the sanctuary. There is the foundation myth of Pelops and Hippodameia: the hero and heroine are brought to life, and as we shall see are also visited and honoured in adjacent shrines at the heart of the sanctuary. Men and athletes can look up at the hero Pelops and emulate his courage: girls can be inspired by the sturdy figure of Hippodameia: her prize was marriage, and the girls' games at Olympia in honour of Hera which she founded are also rites of passage marking transitions towards marriage. Politically, Pelops represents and justifies Elis – who, by eliminating Oinomaos' city of Pisa, has taken charge of the games. At the same time, we are aware that the one ultimately in control is Zeus, both on the pediment and off. As we examine the tableau, we wonder about the judgement and justice of Zeus.

We may then notice the aged man sitting on the ground beyond the horses to the right with a look of faint shock on his face. He and his counterpart on the left represent two prophetic families attached to Olympia from time immemorial, the Iamidai and the Klutidai – a reference to the real shrine and also a device to create questioning in the viewer – What should be thought? What and who is Zeus? – The son of Pelops will be Atreus who served up the cooked children of his brother, Thyestes, and brought down a curse and plenty of murder, as told in Aeschylus' tragedy, *Oresteia*. If this questioning mood sounds unconvincingly modern, it is to be found in the *Agamemnon* of Aeschylus, especially where the puzzled Chorus cry out:

> Zeus – whoever is he? – if
> he answers kindly to the name
> then this I call him – Zeus.
> I have nothing to compare
> weighing in the balance all,
> only Zeus ...
>
> Aeschylus, *Agamemnon* 160-5

Aeschylus wrote this in 458 BC, at just about the time when the temple of Zeus was being finished. What the sculpture offers as comfort to the viewer is a noble and worthy Zeus-figure at the axial point of the scene, probably conceived as invisible or as a statue, since no character reacts to him. Although the story itself arouses discomfort, the nobility and strength of the half-unveiled Zeus figure, and its strong, pivotal position, act as the repetition of the name of Zeus does for the Chorus: it is something to lean on.

The west pediment

As at Delphi, the back pediment features a fight (Fig. 28). The Olympia sculptors have reversed the gods – here Apollo is on the back pediment – the still point of a squirming world. We also have men, women and horse-bodies, but now the fighters are in close contact and violently active.

28. Reconstruction model of the west pediment, temple of Zeus, Olympia.

63

The scene is the battle of Centaurs and Lapiths. Centaurs are half-man, half-horse, their lower half representing the animal nature in man, which can easily lose control: Centaurs can be noble and wise, but often they fail to live up to the Greek ideal of self-control. In this myth, the Greek Lapith hero Peirithous gives a wedding feast for his bride, Deidameia, supported by his best friend, Theseus. At the feast, the Centaurs succumb to drink, and grope the women and young boys. Lapiths fight them off without weapons.

This popular scene may well have reference to the Persians and their recent attack on Greece. (Persians were famed for their horsemanship, so were compared to Centaurs.) However, it can have wider reference. The pediment faces the palaistra area where wrestling and boxing took place – this connection chalks up a positive view of fighting, suitable for an athletics venue. Animal elements can be seen as entirely bad, or as sheer energy in need of control. The fight can be political/historical – or psychological, applicable to everyone – or ascetic, referring to the rigorous physical training undergone by athletes, who must avoid all those pitfalls of drink and other indulgences which have tripped up the centaurs. Or it can be just a fight.

The way in which the groups of fighters on the west pediment are entangled provides an exciting natural-looking scene. However, the design is very carefully worked out so that the sculptures form two exactly balanced groups, one each side of central Apollo who stands (like Zeus on the east) isolated as a pure vertical at the apex. The vertical central figure keys the pediment into the architecture of the façade as a whole; and Apollo (more visibly involved than Zeus), stretches out a horizontal arm to bring order, parallel to the architrave and base. The pediment contains both order and disorder, since the chaotic groups fit the pediment neatly, and exactly balance to left and right. The scene simultaneously presents strife and harmony: strife between the opposing forces of civilisation and animal energy; harmony in response to the unseen god. Apollo is of course the son of Zeus, so acts as an extension of the power of Zeus.

The metopes

A further set of sculptures is found on the metopes within the porches – the Labours of Heracles (Figs 26, 29). Heracles, another son of Zeus, was an interesting choice for the position half in and half out of the temple, since he is the mortal who became a god. Heracles is often represented as slightly comic, devoted to food and drink, slightly animalistic in his lion-skin garment: here he is a purer, nobler figure, genuinely moving in his strong, quiet, patience. As he won immortality through suffering and struggle, he is a wonderful role model for the athletes who will win a brief immortality in victory. On the metopes, Heracles demonstrates a variety of wrestling moves and feats of strength. He also shows that he can suffer

64

and endure, he can use thought and skill and even (in the cleansing of the Augean stables) technology.

Heracles also traditionally founded the foot-race at Olympia in 776 BC. (In the typical way of myth, there are two important foundation stories, but room is made for both.) Many incidents chosen for the Labours take place around the Peloponnese, perhaps in visitors' own homelands. He also descends to Hades to capture Cerberus, the guard-dog, and receives the golden fruit of immortality; these feats give him an appropriate universality.

The twelve Labours of Heracles neatly fit the two sets of six metopes (Fig. 29). Arranged as they are at opposite ends of the huge temple, it is interesting to speculate how far the ancient viewer would have been able to view them as a unity. Looking at the restored drawing we can perceive a pattern. Metopes 1 and 3 of the series include Athene and Hermes; metopes 10, 11 and 12 also include Athene and Hermes. Athene, facing inwards, is the start figure and the finish, bracketing the series. She is the goddess who helps heroes as well as being the daughter of Zeus. The series begins and ends in a similar way, and the designer, it seems, has expected the viewer to remember this over some few minutes while strolling from one end to another.

29. Reconstruction drawing of the Heracles metopes, temple of Zeus, Olympia.

The series also plays with a variety of poses. In scenes of battling with monsters, Heracles stands in action poses, mainly using diagonals. However, in scenes including gods, there is an emphasis on the vertical. When associating with gods, Heracles himself stands vertically and the scene is a peaceful one. Viewed in combination with the architecture, these scenes take on extra resonance, since the building includes the major verticals of the columns and the smaller triple verticals of the triglyphs, which divide the scenes. Two scenes contain three figures, namely scenes 1 and 10. Scene 10, viewed in context, resembles a triglyph, with its two upright immortals and the rigid Heracles between them (Fig. 30). In scene 1, by contrast, Heracles is bowed between the two divinities. Here he has just killed the Nemean lion, and is famously exhausted by his first task – but

30. Heracles metope: Athene, Heracles and Atlas.

by scene 10, he has matured enough to bear up the heavens. When these two scenes are compared, it seems that with maturity, the hero has become a part of sacred architecture, along with gods. If this suggestion is correct, it seems that the designer was indeed confident of the ability of the ancient viewer to make the link by memory without the aid of diagrams and notes.

The ash altar of Olympian Zeus

This was a very different sort of monument from the sophisticated temple, but it must have been the true religious heart of the Altis (Fig. 21).

Pausanias tells us that it lay 'at the same distance from the Pelopeion and the temple of Hera, but further forward than either of them' (Pausanias 5.xiii.8). We would know nothing of it without his *Guide* as it has completely disappeared. The fifth-century temple of Zeus was obviously built in relation to this important altar, but as usual without any formal lining up. Both temples faced it at an angle so it seems to have been acceptable for a temple to face its altar at an angle, rather than symmetrically as might be expected.

The altar was built from ash – reputedly started off by Heracles and so very ancient and sacred (Fig. 23). It was cone-shaped, stepped and circular; the outer circumference, marked by stones, was 125 feet according to Pausanias, and in his time the top reached 22 feet in height. At each sacrifice, the part to be burnt (rather than the part eaten by worshippers) was taken up to the top; and the ashes obtained were saved for the nineteenth day of the Greek month Elaphios, then mixed with Alphaios water and daubed over the altar, increasing its size a little every year. The height and bulk of the altar, composed entirely of pulverised sacrifices, was thus a tangible record of the antiquity of the cult. Girls and women were allowed to climb the stone steps to the first level, but only men could go up to the top.

Hera had her own ash altar near her temple, and so did Earth herself.

The Pelopeion

Two more monuments are important for the meaning of the sanctuary, even though one has scanty remains and the other has vanished. The Pelopeion was a hero shrine of great antiquity. What could be seen was just a low grassy grave mound: in the fifth century (perhaps in association with the building of the temple) this was made more monumental with a surrounding wall in an odd five-sided shape, and a classical propylon. Inside were trees, statues and a mound. Although modern opinion has varied as to whether this 'grave' really had any contents, it is now thought to contain a genuine Bronze Age burial. The connection with Pelops supplies a foundation hero for Olympia and the mound is perhaps the oldest thing at Olympia. Pausanias says that Pelops 'was worshipped more than any other hero at Olympia, just as much as Zeus was worshipped more than any other god' (Pausanias 5.xiii.1).

The quiet but heroic warrior figure already seen on the pediment of the temple of Zeus brought this ancient, buried, foundation hero to life and provided a good role model for the male visitor.

The Hippodameion

The other hero-shrine was for the bride of Pelops – Hippodameia. No trace of this remains, but Pausanias describes it as 'a walled enclosure of a quarter of an acre which women enter once a year to perform rites in honour of Hippodameia and to offer her sacrifice' (Pausanias 6.xx.7).

Plenty of other activities were associated with Hippodameia. As at Athens, a **peplos** was woven every four years for presentation to the goddess: here, it was for Hera. Sixteen married women were chosen for the task. They in turn chose sixteen girls to compete in the Heraia – women's games for Hera, distinct from the Olympic games for men. These included girls' foot-races for three age-groups, run in the same stadium as for men – but one sixth less in length: 'they run with their hair loose, tunic above the knee, and the right breast and shoulder bare' (Fig. 31). Girl-winners of races got crowns of olive, a share of Hera's sacrificial ox and the right to dedicate a painted portrait. These games were said to be founded by Hippodameia herself; although they took place at a separate time from the men's competitions, they could have been an intrinsic part of the games at Olympia from the beginning (Pausanias 5.xvi.1-4). We know that Spartan

31. Bronze figure of a running girl, 520-500 BC. Height: 11.5 cm.

girls did athletics. These Peloponnesian girls were not specified as Spartan, but it seems unlikely that any girls would run a serious race without any training at all – probably sporting activities were a normal part of their education. The Sixteen also arranged dances for Hippodameia; another sixteen women were chosen to 'serve' the Sixteen; altogether many females would have had a chance to be involved, at some time, in some way, in the Heraia. All this suggests more organised activity for women than is often supposed.

The vanished shrine of Hippodameia was extensive and had more of a presence than we might have guessed. The young figure of Hippodameia on the east front of the temple gathers up some real feminine interests, not only the myth and the tomb. It is a focus for girls and women who are interested in marriage, even perhaps an inspiration for some self-motivation. Hippodameia was thwarted in her efforts to move normally from girlhood to marriage, by her perverse and cruel father. Hippodameia (Horsetamer-woman) was active enough to promote her own destiny: she went in the chariot with Pelops, perhaps choosing him as husband. In some versions of the myth, she even took a hand in the defeat of her father. She then founded the Heraia in thanks for her marriage, Hera being goddess of marriage. By partaking in the games, girls would be promoting their own growth from child to adult, a move sometimes considered problematic for either sex by the ancient Greeks. On the pediment, Hippodameia is lifting her dress at the shoulder, a

68

gesture indicating readiness for marriage. The female career is thus catered for at Olympia, and in a more pro-active way than we might have expected.

Oinomaos' pillar

To complete the trio, even wicked King Oinomaos had his memorial. Preserved under a low shelter was a stump of a wooden pillar. A poem on a bronze plaque informed the ancient tourist that this was the remnant of Oinomaos' palace, struck by Zeus' lightning! So the little monument neatly recorded both an ancient king and the justice of Zeus.

Treasuries

Here at Olympia, as at Delphi, there were treasuries. On a raised terrace at the base of the Hill of Kronos, they stood together in an uneven line of eleven, mostly archaic (Fig. 21). At that time, the terrace would have been a good viewing station for the stadium, which was then inside the Altis. However, as the sanctuary developed, more room was required within it, and the stadium was moved eastwards to just outside the Altis. The terrace remains a good vantage point for architectural display.

The treasuries were largely Doric, and they each exemplified the individual characteristics of their own local building styles. For example, the largest, that from Gela in Sicily, had a characteristic terracotta cladding, ornately painted in geometric patterns, which had to be made and brought from the homeland in Sicily. As at Delphi, each treasury was like a stall at an international fair, advertising the value and uniqueness of its own polis or city-state, in company and to some extent in competition with others.

The Nike of Paionios

One of the many statues once crowding the Altis was so monumental as almost to compete with the buildings. A huge winged Victory descends upon a ten-metre pyramidal column, topped by the beak of a ship (Fig. 32). The artistic point of the sculpture is to make a mass of marble appear to land with feather-lightness from the air, while spread wings and billowing garments swirl upward in the windy wake of the goddess. An eagle under her feet may be a courtesy nod to Zeus, since the monument was directly opposite his temple, and the goddess herself reminds us of the golden **Nike** held by the chryselephantine Zeus.

Victory was naturally a theme at Olympia. The Nike of Paionios recorded the victory of the Messenians and Naupactians over the Spartans (420 BC). Its inscription continues: 'Paionios made this and was victorious

32. The Nike of Paionios, Olympia, *c.* 420 BC.

... in winning the commission for the temple acroteria', adding the concept of artistic contest to the other forms: military and athletic.

Of the hundreds of statues which Pausanias tells us once crowded Olympia, sadly few are left. Of life-size marble, there is this Nike and the Hermes of Praxiteles, and all the sculptures from the temple, happily preserved by the flood mud of Alphaios and Kladeos. Almost everything else has fallen prey to chance, to the sophisticated Roman collector, or to the unsophisticated melter of bronze or recycler of marble.

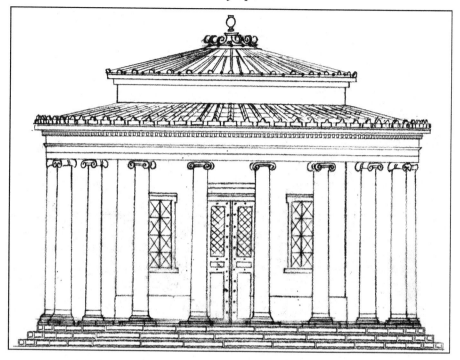

33. Reconstruction drawing of the Philippeion, Olympia, shown with a stepped roof.

The Philippeion

As at Delphi, outsiders could gain prestige by making showy offerings at a famous Pan-Hellenic shrine. One such building would have been very noticeable, tucked just within the Altis area, behind the Heraion and Pelopeion and almost against the boundary (Fig. 21). It has even been suggested that the temenos wall was diverted here to make space for it. The Philippeion was a tholos of stone and marble in Ionic style (Fig. 33), started sometime after 338 BC by Philip of Macedon to mark his final victory over the Greeks at the battle of Chaeronea, and eventually finished after his death by his son Alexander the Great.

The outer colonnade of eighteen columns was Ionic, and supported a plain frieze topped by dentils. The roof was marble, probably in two steps, and conical, crowned by a bronze poppy-head. Pausanias tells us it was built of brick and marble. In fact, it had marble columns and a marble dado base to the cella wall: above that was limestone, stuccoed and painted to imitate brick. The cella, lit by two windows, was decorated inside with nine engaged Corinthian columns, one corresponding to each alternate exterior column space.

The building might count as a treasury – a cross between a temple and a storehouse. Yet it is placed, not among the treasuries, but on the edge of the temple area. And the statues it housed represented no god of the sanctuary, but were full-height family portrait sculptures of Philip, his parents, his queen Olympias and Alexander their son, all grouped on a crescent-shaped plinth and sculpted by Leochares, a highly-regarded Greek sculptor (Pausanias 5.xx.9-10).

The presence of this monument shows the power of Macedon at the time. Although non-Greeks could make offerings at Pan-Hellenic shrines – for example, Croesus King of Lydia had loved to enrich Delphi – this particular offering would seem to make certain claims. The statues were chryselephantine – just like the adjacent Zeus. Votive statues of winning athletes were marble or bronze, girl victors dedicated paintings only: in the hierarchy of materials, chryselephantine was for divinity. Possibly even more offensive to some was the use of Ionic style and the combination of an Attic frieze with dentils: did this amount to a claim to be 'spiritually' Athenian? The Macedonians were not considered by the Greeks to be really Greeks (although they claimed they were), and anyway Philip was an invader and occupier of Greece. The choice of a round building in Ionic style made sure of catching attention in a mainly Doric mainland site. Additionally, this Olympic tholos, more exotic than its Doric competitor at Delphi, evened up the architectural score.

The Echo Stoa and the stadium

This stoa ran 100 metres from north to south, separating the Altis from the stadium area (Fig. 21). It had a double corridor, divided by an Ionic interior colonnade; the exterior was Doric. Paintings decorated its back wall and an echo gave it its name. Stoas provided a civilised place to meet, and also to set out stalls and do business, all in the welcome shade. This stoa was well-placed to provide a useful multi-purpose amenity in the centre of the Altis. It also gave definition to the different areas, the Altis and the sports area.

The stadium is now outside the most sacred area of the Altis although it started off within it. It was and still is mainly an earth construction, as Pausanias describes, taking advantage of natural contours of the ground. It accommodated 45,000 spectators and was 212.5 metres long, 28.5 metres wide.

On the central south side there were stone seats for the presidents of the games and opposite this point on the other side was a 'white stone altar on which a married woman sits, the priestess of Demeter'. Pausanias adds surprisingly: 'Virgin girls of course are not barred from watching' (Pausanias 6.xx.8-9), although elsewhere we learn that married women were barred on pain of death except for the priestess herself, who was married. Pausanias, writing in the second century AD, may be misleading us about the classical era: as athletes competed in the nude, there would be reason to ban women from attending.

The stadium is still reached through a long masonry passage that was once a barrel-vaulted tunnel called the Hidden Entrance. Through this, the judges and athletes could make a dramatic appearance. In front of the treasuries and leading to the Hidden Entrance is the row of thirteen plinths for the Zanes: these were bronze statues of Zeus, paid for by fines exacted from athletes found cheating.

Later, there was a separate course for chariot racing and horse events, the hippodrome.

Other buildings

The early fifth-century **Prytaneion** just within the Altis was a useful building for officials and VIP hospitality. It contained a sacred hearth and an eternal flame.

Just outside the Altis, many other functional buildings were gradually added. The palaistra (third century) and gymnasium (second century) would have been appreciated for their shady colonnades; before they were built, the activities they housed – boxing, wrestling, etc., would have been carried on in some more informal setting, perhaps on roughly the same sites. Colonnades provided shade for philosophical discussion as well as athletic activity. Other amenities such as baths would have been equally appreciated: Greek-style baths were built in the early fifth century; the rivers offered washing places in earlier times. The **Leonidaion**, donated in the late fourth century BC by Leonidas of Naxos, was a generous addition to the comfort of their stay for superior guests. It was a 'hotel' built in a square around a garden courtyard and containing numerous bedrooms, rather like a modern motel.

The **Bouleuterion** or council chamber just outside the Altis was a double building of archaic horseshoe plan. One of the two linked sections was an authentically archaic council-house – the other was a fifth-century reproduction in archaic style! Between the two was the important statue of Zeus Horkios ('of oaths') where athletes swore to follow the rules.

Conclusion

The sanctuary of Olympia operated successfully for over a thousand years. It continued to be developed well into Roman times (though here we have only looked at buildings up to the fifth century BC). The site was extraordinarily well-chosen for access and attractiveness, as proved by the success and fame of the games. It must also have been extremely well-run considering the huge numbers attending and competing. Visitors today still find the site seductively pleasant – some echo of the senior Greek games festival still lingers on in a lasting holiday mood.

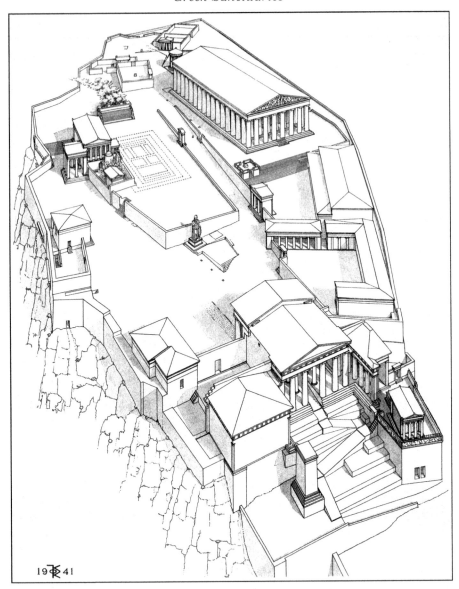

19 41

34. Reconstruction view of the Athenian Acropolis from the west; clockwise from front: Propylaia, House of the Arrhephoroi, Erechtheion, ruins of 'old Athene temple', Parthenon, Khalkotheke, sanctuary of Artemis Brauronia, sanctuary of Athene Nike.

7

The Athenian Acropolis: historical background

The Acropolis is, even today, a startling city-centre feature rising abruptly to a height of well over 100 metres from street-level (Fig. 71). It is a natural limestone outcrop with steep cliffs on all sides but the west; its sloping summit has to some extent been squared off with infill and terracing; its upper sides have been clad with sheer fortress-like walls. In the lower slopes are found natural caves, many adapted as shrines. There are also springs and fountains at this level, approachable from above: this vital feature led to its early adoption as a defensible habitation. The top of the rock is an elongated sloping plateau, measuring very roughly 270 x 156 metres.

In Mycenaean times, the Acropolis seems to have had an unremarkable history. Towards the end of the period, around 1300-1200 BC, it acquired a palace complete with substantial terracing, and was then encircled by Cyclopean walls, including a propylon on the western slope.

Following the collapse of the Mycenaean 'palace civilisation', the Athenians lived in an undistinguished way around and sometimes on this natural fortress for centuries. Their subsequent rise to prominence was reflected in the buildings that eventually came to adorn it. Two distinct periods are represented in architecture: the archaic and the classical. They are sharply divided by the year 480/79 in which invading Persians systematically destroyed what was already built, leaving the site – in a sense – cleared for future development.

This is the site and the opportunity that Pericles later exploited so successfully (Figs 34, 35).

The archaic era: from tyranny to democracy

During the sixth century the Acropolis was developed with many buildings and votive sculptures. After the destruction of the site by the Persians in 480/79, damaged sculptures were buried in pits. Excavation has brought these to light, demonstrating the richness of the archaic Acropolis. However it has proved difficult to assign the architectural fragments to particular buildings or locations. Constant redevelopment of the sanctuary has obliterated precise traces of the past.

Politically the sixth century was also one of change. There were class struggles and vigorous attempts to establish an equitable legal system. In 540, Peisistratus seized power as tyrant (unconstitutional ruler) and was

75

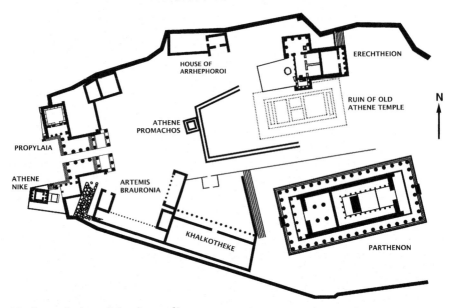

35. Ground plan of the Acropolis.

succeeded by his son in 527. The Peisistratid dynasty did many things to enhance the life and the culture of the city, but Hippias, the son, eventually became very unpopular and in 510 he was ousted with the military help of Sparta.

By 507, a democracy was organised in Athens. Democracy was 'the rule of all the citizens' – which in practice meant all Athenian males of qualifying age and status (not, of course, foreigners, slaves or women). With this proviso, the citizens of Athens had a remarkable degree of access to the processes of government. Most officials were chosen by lot annually. The *boule* (deliberative council) was a revolving group of 500, chosen by lot; their meeting place was in the Agora. The *ekklesia* (full assembly) was for every qualifying male to attend; there he could voice his opinion if he wished and could give his vote as a matter of duty. This assembly met on a hill called the Pnyx which overlooked the Agora and faced the Acropolis.

The Athenians rejoiced at this change from the rule of one man, however enlightened and benign. They reckoned a system where every citizen had his own voice in government – and had equality before the law – a civic possession of infinite value.

Archaic buildings on the Acropolis: 'Bluebeard' and the 'old Athene temple'

The Peisistratids are often credited with important building programmes on the Acropolis, but it is uncertain which, if any, they really undertook. In the period 570-550 there was a great deal of activity, clustering around

76

the introduction of the quadrennial festival, the Greater Panathenaia, in 566/5. During these years, dozens of statues were offered by individuals, the western access ramp was enlarged, and a sizeable limestone temple was built whose pediments (now in the Acropolis Museum) featured ferocious lions and a strange 'Bluebeard' figure. It is not known where this temple stood, whether on the Mycenaean terracing or possibly on the site later used for the Parthenon.

Towards the end of the sixth century another limestone temple was built on the Acropolis whose foundations can be clearly seen today. It took up some of the space once occupied by the Mycenaean palace, and was sited on its ancient terracing for impressive effect. This temple was built to house the ancient cult statue of Athene Polias (protectress of the city), and must have replaced whatever temple already did that important job, whether the 'Bluebeard' or a yet older one. Again, it is not known whether the Peisistratids were the patrons of this grand late-archaic building, or whether it was built to celebrate the new democracy – or even was adopted half-built and completed by the democracy. Some of the marble pedimental sculpture can be seen in the Acropolis Museum: Athene dispatches giants; possibly Zeus arrives in his chariot. A similar Gigantomachy was probably on the west end of the Alcmaeonid temple at Delphi; it seems the two Athenian-influenced temples should be related to each other, but it is still unclear which is earlier.

The fifth century: from the burning of Sardis to the building of the Parthenon

War and the threat of war with Persia dominated the first half of the fifth century BC for the Greek city-states generally. Athens in particular was a target for the Persians right from the beginning. This was because of her special relationship with the Ionian Greek city-states and island-states which bordered the Persian empire along the eastern Mediterranean coastline (see map on p. xii). Persia's enormous and expanding empire already included a vast interior land mass, ending at the coast.

Traditionally and mythically the Ionian city-states were offshoots of Athens. When the Ionian cities felt increasingly threatened by Persia, it made sense for them to approach the Athenians, who were persuaded to play an unwise and dangerous game; they joined the Ionians in a military expedition to the Persian interior, and in 499/8 they captured and burnt Sardis. Herodotus (*Histories* 5.104) tells how the roofs of that city were all of flammable thatch; accidentally, the temple of Cybele was destroyed. This insult explains why the Persians were later so very particular to destroy every temple on the Acropolis.

Persia's ambitions apparently included the absorption of the whole of Greece. The invasion of the mainland began with the famous landing at Marathon in 490, under the guidance of old Hippias, the exiled Peisistratid tyrant. Had it been successful, Hippias would have become the puppet king and Athens would have lost her treasured new democracy along with her freedom.

The battle of Marathon was the 'miraculous' event in which the terrifying invading power was defeated by a citizen army half the size. The casualty figures recorded by the Greeks were: 6,400 Persians slain on the field of battle to only 192 Athenians. Heroes and gods were observed to fight for the Athenians: Pan, Theseus and Heracles were all present. On the field of battle a mound was raised in Homeric style for the burial of the slain heroes. The victory was the iconic event of the new Athenian democracy. In commemoration, a great new marble temple was begun on the south side of the Acropolis – the Marathon temple.

Salamis

Not everyone believed that lasting victory was achieved. Sure enough, the Persians were planning a return – which happened in 480/79. The invaders reached Attica, encamped on the Areopagos, penetrated the Acropolis and deliberately threw down or burnt everything which they found up there, the huge Mycenaean fortification wall, the dedicated statues and the temples, including the partly-built Marathon temple.

But the Persians were destroying an abandoned city. After Marathon, Themistocles had persuaded the Athenians to build up their fleet, as he believed that sea-power was the way to withstand Persia. When it was known that the Persians were actually on their way back to Greece, the Athenians sent to Delphi for advice: they were told: 'Seek safety in the wooden walls.' A few diehards interpreted this as the wooden planking forming part of the Acropolis gateway. They stayed to defend the Acropolis and were slaughtered as they took refuge in the 'old temple'. But most were convinced by Themistocles that the 'wooden walls' were the new ships, standing ready for an emergency such as this. The priestess of Athene Polias backed him, pointing out that the sacred snake had already deserted the Acropolis, a powerful omen.

The whole population of Athens (apart from those few diehards) evacuated the city, carrying with them the sacred image of Athene Polias. It certainly was a bold strategy: the women and children were placed in safety in Troezen and Salamis. The men manned the ships at Salamis, visible from the Acropolis. Proactive Themistocles even manipulated the battle, tricking the Persians into attacking in a space far too narrow for their large ships to manoeuvre in. They were trapped and became sitting targets for the battle-rams of the more versatile Athenian triremes. Once again, Pan was seen to fight for the Athenians. The battle was a triumph for democracy against tyranny and barbarism.

Insofar as a city is 'men not walls', Athens was gloriously safe. However, the built city, Athens, especially the Acropolis with all its memorials of history, was now a wreck. All the temples, all the beautiful statues dedicated to Athene were broken and spoilt. Also, although the Persians had been beaten back, they were a great power, angry, shamed and hostile. They might return.

The Delian League

Athens, glorious victor of Salamis, then made an offer to the rest of the Greeks. Any city-state which felt itself too small to build up a navy of its own could contribute yearly ship-money to Athens. Athens would use it to build and maintain a naval force sufficient to protect them all. This would mainly be of interest to city-states and island states bordering the Persian territory and in the Eastern Mediterranean. It was an offer that small and vulnerable cities could scarcely afford to refuse: its effect was to give Athens almost imperial power.

The money raised would be kept on the sacred island of Delos, hence the name of the scheme. By 454, the leader, Pericles, had transferred these funds to Athens. The Delian League worked very well in that Athens did successfully police the Ionian Sea, until the Persians finally agreed on a truce or treaty in 449. It also meant that Athens now had enormous resources. Following the truce, Pericles saw fit to propose the rebuilding of the Acropolis sanctuary.

The oath of Plataea

It is said that the Greeks – or perhaps just the Athenians – swore an oath during the war with Persia known as the oath of Plataea, in which they promised 'not to rebuild any of the temples burnt and ruined by the Persian, but to leave them as a testimony to future generations of the impiety of the barbarian'. This oath is recorded by two rather later ancient writers (Diodorus and Lycurgus) and it is not known for certain whether it is authentic. Plutarch makes no reference to it when discussing Pericles' plans for a Pan-Hellenic conference on the rebuilding of the sanctuaries throughout Greece, and it may be that the oath was invented later to explain the fact of the delay in rebuilding.

For whatever reason, it seems that the Acropolis, ruined by the Persians, was left in ruins for 30 years without any significant new architectural projects, although the Athenians must have tidied up sufficiently to be able to carry on the cult activity, and to shelter their precious Athene Polias, and probably an Athene Nike (Victory) as well. What else was done within the sanctuary is unclear.

The defensive walls around the city were rebuilt straightaway – swiftly and haphazardly, with whatever material was to hand. Even parts of damaged sculptures and inscriptions were re-used simply as useful and available stone material.

On the Acropolis, the north wall was rebuilt in an unusual way: architectural elements were used, but not haphazardly. Column drums and triglyphs were arranged, each in a line, in a correct relationship to each other (Fig. 73). This wall is the one clearly seen from the Agora, the main public space of the city. This deliberate display of salvaged temple parts was highly visible, and tellingly reminded everybody of 'the impiety of the barbarians'.

Pericles

Pericles was a leader of the 'popular' party who held outstanding influence in the Athenian democracy increasingly from about 461 till his death in 429. It was he who proposed the re-modelling of the ruined Acropolis with buildings which would reflect Athens' own pride in herself and her new position among the Greek city-states. For this purpose, he moved the funds of the Delian League from Delos to Athens. Despite criticism from various quarters he pushed ahead with a major scheme which did in fact give both pleasure and widespread employment to the citizens, and ever since has reflected fame upon Athens, just as Pericles hoped.

When the buildings of the Acropolis sanctuary were half completed, alliance between the Greek city-states broke down due to the increasing power of Athens and resulting aggression from Sparta. These two cities were the major leaders in Greece, Sparta being supreme in the 'Dorian' mainland, Athens having her Ionian allies. The resulting war – the Peloponnesian War, 431- 404 BC – was especially horrible, as it was Greeks against Greeks. It lasted on and off for the rest of the fifth century and weakened both sides permanently. Pericles was the leader of Athens during the first part of the war but soon died. His Acropolis building programme seems to have been carried out more or less in its entirety, being continued after his death, despite the terrible conditions such as plague and disastrous defeats.

Something of Pericles' vision of Athens is glimpsed in his Funeral Speech for the fallen in 431-430, the first year of the war with Sparta, as recorded by Thucydides. In this speech Pericles is represented as praising Athens for her open and equal society. He contrasts Athens with her Dorian opponents, rejoicing that Athens is a well-rounded society in which aesthetics and qualities of the intellect can be valued without any loss of physical courage. Of course, Sparta was well-known as a military state in which citizens were under constant surveillance, and the restrictive constitution was purely aimed at preserving the status quo.

Pericles claimed that in contrast: '... We [Athenians] choose to face danger in a relaxed way rather than with a painful regime, and to trust more in our naturally courageous character than in state regulations ... We love beauty yet are not extravagant, and we love wisdom yet are not soft ...' (Thucydides, *History* 2.39)

7. The Athenian Acropolis: historical background

The sturdy Doric style prevalent in mainland Greece represents the manly character which Pericles here claims for his citizens: yet the elegant Ionic style originating from the east Mediterranean represents those cultural values which Athens also embraced. On the Acropolis, these two styles will be seen combined in a perfect blend, mirroring the perfect city.

8

The Parthenon

The Parthenon was the first of the great Periclean structures: the 'flag-ship' of the whole programme (Fig. 36). The Parthenon is unique, yet appears to be 'the classic Greek temple'. Its fame puts it frequently before the public eye. Familiarity creates acceptance: yet, almost everything about the Parthenon is different, and the competitiveness expressed by Greek buildings should lead us to anticipate this.

36. Reconstruction view of the Parthenon.

The platform

A foundation for a great temple on the south side of the Acropolis plateau was prepared shortly after 490, to commemorate Marathon. The rock itself was stable and strong, but a huge amount of preparation had had to be done in order to lift a flat building-surface to the highest part of the rock profile. This had entailed building a massive retaining wall parallel to the southern edge of the hill, and then infilling back to the desired level. (It is possible that older foundations of an archaic temple underlie the Mara-thon platform, but this is uncertain.)

Despite the Persian damage done to the partly-built Marathon temple in 480/79, the foundation platform was still perfectly good and could be used again. But, by 447, its proportion was not acceptable, being too long and too narrow. To create the classical effect, as seen at Olympia, the platform had to be made wider, and a small amount of the length had to be wasted.

Expanding the temple to the north not only modernised the proportions but also allowed the temple to be seen from the Agora. The modification was simple: only normal foundations were required because the rocky ground was already high enough on this side.

The Doric Parthenon

The Parthenon is overwhelmingly a Doric temple, though with Ionic influences and details. At a quick glance it resembles the temple of Zeus at Olympia, but there are many differences.

The Parthenon had a lower pediment with a flatter angle, so despite its slightly larger footprint, the overall height was much the same. The flattened pediment appears more elegant and less dominant.

The standard three steps of the new Parthenon platform are, like those of the temple of Zeus, too large to ascend by stepping. Where the Olympia temple has a ramp, the Parthenon designers opted for intermediate steps – a neater solution.

The temple of Zeus is hexastyle, the Parthenon is octostyle. This is unusual for Doric, but not unique. (The early archaic temple of Artemis at Corcyra was octostyle and so was a late archaic temple at Selinus.) It should be noted that a frontage of eight columns does not necessarily create a larger temple than one with six. The Parthenon is slightly larger but the columns are more slender: Zeus' more massive columns each take up more room.

The Parthenon is 30.88 x 69.5 metres; the temple of Zeus is 27.7 x 64.1 metres. It is clear from these measurements that the comparatively small increase in footprint is deliberately competitive. Both temples are colossal and impressive on a very similar scale. Considering that the Parthenon's pre-built foundation would have allowed for a longer temple, while it was actually decided to create a broader but shorter temple, it is clear that the uppermost ideas in the designers' minds were first to achieve an up-to-date classical proportion, and secondly to cap the size of the rival temple at Olympia. The Parthenon does create an effect of enormous size. Its position on the crest of a hill, and in a relatively small-scale site, increases this effect. The temple of Zeus used more massive detailed proportions, such as the heavy columns, the more imposing pediment. Its low-lying and spacious site worked towards an effect of strength, weight and solidity. In

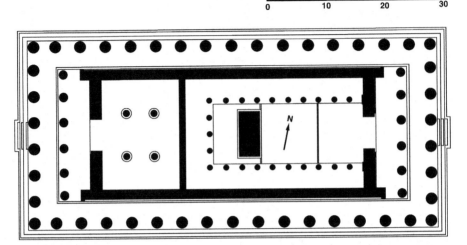

37. Ground plan of the Parthenon.

contrast, the slimly-styled Parthenon, first viewed against the sky, appears airy and weightless.

To achieve a classical ground plan, the Parthenon uses a version of the 'Zeus formula': double the number of façade columns plus one more results in 8 x 17 columns (Fig. 37).

The Parthenon column style is, of course, high classical (Fig. 38): the round echinus is shallow, taut and compact; the square abacus fits neatly upon it, just overlapping the architrave edge above. The shaft appears straight, but is gently tapered with a subtle entasis. The column base is almost the same diameter as the echinus.

The slim columns were (as far as possible) reclaimed material from the hundreds of drums already prepared for the Marathon temple. The sensible economy resulted in a design triumph. The easy workability of the local Pentelic marble also helped; at Olympia, the designers had to work within the limitations of shelly limestone.

The entablature has the standard Doric arrangement of blank architrave, with triglyph and metope frieze above. All 92 metopes are carved in deep relief and both pediments have sculptured compositions of many free-standing over-life-size marble figures (discussed below).

Porches

The inner porches of the Parthenon are hexastyle prostyle (Fig. 37). Most Doric temples have their inner porches distyle in antis, e.g. the large-scale temple of Zeus at Olympia. The benefit of this for Zeus was a large spacious area to give importance to the temple door, to display the porch sculpture, to

8. The Parthenon

38. North-east corner of the Parthenon entablature.

be enjoyed as a viewing platform. In the Parthenon, the priority has been given not to space but to a multiplicity of columns. The prostyle porch columns are scaled smaller than those of the outer colonnade, and are raised on two steps.

Interior

Inside, the Parthenon was divided into two unequal non-communicating chambers. The eastern chamber, facing the rising sun, was the cella intended for the statue of the goddess. The western chamber, sometimes called the 'Parthenon' (maiden's chamber), or opisthodomos, was a 'strong-room' for storing treasure. Each chamber had its own porch entrance.

The eastern chamber unusually had two windows flanking the splendid door. It had the now usual double colonnade of two-storey Doric columns, with the difference that behind the statue plinth, the colonnade returned on itself, creating a U-shape. The cella was unusually wide – this was achieved by making the exterior colonnade unusually narrow. This scheme was the opposite to that of Zeus at Olympia where the cella was narrow, the outer colonnade spacious. Pheidias himself, sculptor of the Parthenos statue, friend of Pericles and, according to Plutarch, artistic director of the whole Acropolis programme, was presumably present at the planning stage: it seems likely that he requested extra interior space to surround his projected Athene statue. The effect would be the opposite of that later achieved by his oversized Zeus – a goddess comfortably standing in a spacious interior, bathed in light.

Roof

The roof was tiled in marble. The acroteria were about three metres high and may have been a central floral motif with corner nikai. On each corner were lion-head water-spouts, while the usual palmette antefixes enriched the long sides.

The ceilings would have been all coffered, wooden on the inside and marble along the colonnades and porches, since this was fairly standard on a grand building.

Refinements

'Refinements' is the term for all the many ways in which a Greek temple can deliberately avoid straight lines, right angles and mathematical regularity. Refinements are typical of Doric style and are not generally found in Ionic. As well as tapering and entasis of columns, there are curvatures of surface and many variations on the expected regularity. Tapering and entasis can already be found in archaic temples such as the temple of Apollo at Corinth and can be rather obvious, even crude. Here on the Parthenon, in its most developed form, the use of the system is so subtle it is almost imperceptible:

- Starting with the stylobate or platform on which the columns rest, the overall surface is very gently convex, as are the lower steps. This upward curve is mirrored in the architrave and cornices of the pediment.
- The architraves, cornices and steps are not actually cut to a curve; they are jointed at imperceptible angles so that an overall faint curve is achieved. This still meant that the jointing of every single stone had to be considered and worked to ensure a tight fit and perfect finish.
- All columns are tilted slightly inwards; the corner columns tilt slightly inwards at an adjusted angle to blend with both façade and flank. Famously the columns have been calculated to meet if projected a mile into the air.
- The columns are not only tilted and tapered with a curve (entasis); the flutes are flatter and wider at the base and gradually narrow and increase in depth till sharper arrises create more shadows at the top.
- The corner columns are very slightly thicker than the others. Vitruvius tells us this is to counteract the effects of light, which 'eats' into the profile of the silhouetted corner column. However, a thicker column would also subtly suggest more strength just where psychologically needed, on the corner.

86

- The corner columns were not only slightly thicker but were also placed slightly closer to their neighbour, reducing the **intercolumniation**. This too would add to the impression of strength and would be pleasing. This is known as corner-contraction.
- The 'triglyph problem' comes into play here. Vitruvius criticises the Doric order because of this intrinsic difficulty. A Doric frieze must end with a triglyph on the corner. However, as triglyphs are also supposed to be centred over columns and intercolumniations, there is a logical problem. So a little juggling has to take place, moving the end-column in slightly and spreading the triglyph-metope arrangement until the triglyph reaches the corner (Figs 38, 44). Visually this works very well. It too is part of corner-contraction.

What these refinements mean in terms of construction is a separate calculation and adjustment for every column, according to its place in the building, and for every apparently straight line in the whole building. The extra cost of shaving the marble surfaces to the exact desired fit must have been considerable. What were the gains?

Drainage has been put forward as an advantage of a sloping floor, and this is clearly a sensible point. However, it does not account for the rest of the system. Looking at the size of the Parthenon, it is clear that such a huge building based on rigid geometry could easily become mechanical and therefore ungainly and ugly. Aesthetic concerns must have been the main factor in this expensive effort.

Visually, because of entasis, the columns seem to react to the weight placed upon them, like toned muscles. An almost organic effect is achieved by the refinements, as though the building were a living entity. There is also a kind of false perspective: the tapering and inclination suggest a greater height without mass. Such optical effects enhance a style of building so dependent on columns.

The Greek word for the outer colonnade of a temple is *pteron* – 'wing'. One desirable effect of an open colonnade is that the building feels light – the roof almost seems to be floating. The Parthenon, placed on a rocky height, appears with its subtle curvature to have just alighted, or to be poised for flight. It appears strong but not heavy, live weight, not dead weight.

As mentioned above, refinements are an integral feature of Doric style and certainly contradict any impression that Doric is crude or mechanical. The Parthenon is the most extreme example of the use of 'refinements'; this is not only due to the ambition of the project but also is a function of its huge size, the unprecedented number of columns, and the need to achieve the elegance appropriate to a goddess.

The Ionic Parthenon

Many things about the Parthenon are Ionic. To begin with, the all-marble building was common in Ionia but not on the Greek mainland. The mainland precedent for an all-marble building was the Siphnian Treasury of imported island marble and also the Athenians' own treasury at Delphi. A building the size of the Parthenon could scarcely have been built in imported marble because of the enormous expense. Luckily for Athens, there was beautiful and plentiful marble available from Mount Pentelicon, only about fifteen kilometres away.

Looking again at the temple of Hera at Samos (Fig. 5) one can see that a characteristic of a full-blown Ionic temple was the 'forest of columns' effect. Columns were slender and lofty, typically eight or more across the façade. Behind those might be eight more creating a dipteral or even tripteral formation. Additionally there might be an inner porch, two or three more columns deep.

The Parthenon, while remaining absolutely within the parameters of Doric style, has manipulated the possibilities of Doric to create this 'forest' effect. Columns proliferate, especially at the short ends where the hexastyle prostyle porch is combined with the octostyle front (Fig. 36). All the columns in their slenderness are 'influenced' by Ionic proportion; a mass of heavy Doric could not have been so appealing.

The continuous frieze running around the cella wall exterior is of course Ionic (Fig. 39). Zeus at Olympia had the Heracles metopes in the porches. The Parthenon extends this idea by extravagantly continuing the frieze down the sides of the temple. Above the frieze ran a plain Doric hawksbeak moulding, painted with a colourful pattern: a piece of this with the pattern plainly visible is in the British Museum. Below the frieze were the guttae and mutules that properly belong under a triglyph frieze. This might be a clue that a triglyph frieze was originally intended. But equally it may be yet another ingenious way of mixing the two orders – a Doric-Ionic or Attic frieze. There is an aesthetic gain too: the neat guttae and mutules do not detract from the refined masterpiece of carving above. This is especially useful because of the sharp angle of viewing; owing to the high location of the frieze the line of sight has to pass the lower border to reach the frieze.

Another good reason for an Ionic frieze may have been precedent. The ruined 'old Athene temple' probably had an Ionic porch frieze. If so, the Parthenon would preserve this memory, while also going one better, since a continuous frieze in the corridor surrounding a Doric cella was new.

In the Parthenon chamber or opisthodomos, four slender space-saving Ionic columns supported the ceiling (Fig. 37). Double-storey Doric columns could have been used, as in the cella, but since the room probably housed the treasure of the Delian League, there was a wry appropriateness in using Ionic.

39. Parthenon frieze, metopes and pediment.

The metopes, 447-442 BC

The metopes were, as usual, the earliest of the sculptures; they had to be inserted into position between triglyphs above the architrave of the outer colonnade before the building could be continued. There were 92 carved metopes on the Parthenon, an unprecedented number, and it is well known that the quality of the carving varied. The metopes which remain intact are mostly from the south side – the least frequented side, being away from both the entrances and the processional north walk; they could therefore have been allotted to the least well-regarded of the sculpting teams. In contrast, the one metope remaining on the north side (in fact on the north-west corner which would be the first approached by a visitor) is probably the most beautiful of all that remain.

The south metopes mainly featured a Centauromachy (Battle of Lapiths and Centaurs); (the subject of the central section is still controversial). The sculptural style is not unlike that of the temple of Zeus: clean-cut, unfussy, rather severe. However even non-experts can detect that different hands have been at work. It is also possible to detect new stylistic tendencies which will be developed as the temple progresses: a softness of facial type and fluidity of drapery, seen in full glory on the pediments.

The carving uses varying depths of relief, with some limbs completely in the round, standing away from the background. They even partially protrude from the surface of the architecture and catch the light, lending drama to the action and liveliness to the face of the temple.

The designers of the south metopes had to invent many combinations of man and horse-body in various wrestling grips. The whole series would have built up an effect of simultaneous cartoon-like movement along a regular geometrically framed strip. A glance at the great length of a Parthenon flank colonnade with its seventeen columns makes very clear that some visual relief would be thought desirable. The decision to 'overload' with sculpture has definitely some purpose to it after all.

The metopes on the other three sides are known to have featured: north, scenes from the Fall of Troy (Ilioupersis); west, Athenians fighting Amazons (Amazonomachy); east, Gods fighting Giants (Gigantomachy). This last topic revived a pediment theme from the 'old Athene temple'. The great feats of Athene in the Gigantomachy were woven each year into her presentation peplos; probably they were the focus of the Panathenaic ritual, so this theme was very appropriate for the entrance front. All the topics signify a struggle for the victory of the good.

The frieze, 442-438 BC

The metopes were unusual for their number, the frieze for its length (160 x 1 metres). With the frieze, the Parthenon sculptors seem to have found their unique style. To the layperson, the frieze would appear to have been carved by a single hand: only experts detect differences. Many aspects are remarkable, including continuity of narrative, variation in pace and incident, drama achieved with a very shallow depth of carving, and overall naturalism and grace. Quite apart from any Ionic associations, an excellent reason for replacing metopes with a continuous frieze can be found. The staccato effect of metopes, each one self-contained and mostly expressing struggle, could become wearisome. The frieze is the diametric opposite of struggle: it expresses co-operation. In the frieze, the citizen body appears united, expressed visually by similarity of type and mood, and the overlapping style. Old and young, woman and man, man and animal, are all intent on one purpose; as one city they worship Athene.

There is widespread agreement that the frieze broadly represents the Panathenaic procession, the main event of the Athenian year. However, there are many variations of this idea and other theories too, since the images do not exactly fit what is known about the Panathenaia. The figures are clearly idealised, for example in their nudity and their perfection, whether they stand for contemporary, historical or even mythical Athenians.

8. The Parthenon

The Parthenon frieze was glimpsed best through columns, giving a stop-start effect as the viewer walked forward at ground level outside the temple (Fig. 39). It is uncertain how clearly it could have been seen, but the white marble floor would certainly have thrown up reflected light and the marble ceiling would have added downward light. The limiting factors for viewing would not have been illumination so much as the great height and the sharp viewing angle. Today much of the frieze is on show in the British Museum and can be closely examined. Originally, extra clarity would have been added by the painted colour-contrast background, and the painted details of faces and clothes.

The movement of the frieze is orchestrated according to the anticipated movement of the viewer. The west end (which is – from a worship point of view – the back) is where a viewer might be expected to pause as he takes in his first close-up view of the temple – and here the frieze-procession also is beginning to gather itself together (Fig. 40); young men prepare to mount their horses. The long sides are where the visitor might be expected to walk faster to reach the front of the temple – here in the frieze-procession, the cavalry is seen to gallop (Fig. 41), and some high-speed competitive games are included, involving chariots. As the viewer approaches the liturgical front and the proximity to Athene Parthenos herself, he will become more worshipful. Boys are seen carefully carrying ritual water-pots and animals are led to sacrifice.

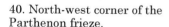
40. North-west corner of the Parthenon frieze.

91

41. Horsemen on the Parthenon frieze.

Finally, on the east front, the procession slows to a standstill. Maidens and elders (Fig. 42) appear as a prelude to the seated gods (Fig. 43). Like the east metopes, the east frieze introduces immortals. This section is arranged in a more architectonic style than the rest. The maidens, who walk so sedately that their robes are not displaced, are like fluted columns. The seated gods, in their organised ranks of six-a-side, frame both the real portal and the mysterious sculpted central ritual. Here, the stools provide insistent horizontals and verticals. There is a sense of calm and revelation as the frieze grows more formal.

The patterned composition using repeated stools and conversing gods with level heads is a clear quotation from the Siphnian Treasury. Why would the Parthenon designers borrow like this? Is it plagiarism? If Ionic style is to be used, then it should consciously cap any previous example –

42. Maidens on the Parthenon frieze.

8. The Parthenon

43. Seated gods on the Parthenon frieze.

according to the Greek spirit of competition and vying for excellence. These fifth-century designers have added classical naturalism and grace to their archaic model, and they have improved the layout by making it symmetrical; they must have objected to the rather odd Siphnian arrangement of adjacent scenes. Here, a comparison with the archaic work seems openly invited.

Each corner of the frieze has an upright accent like a 'bracket' to finish the design in a controlled and architectonic way. Such devices remind us that – however lifelike the frieze – we are actually looking at a building, a stone structure, a temple (Fig. 40).

Another essential trick is the manipulation of scale. Men are as tall as horses, but mounted men are the same height. When it comes to the seated gods, their heads too fit nicely within the border. Gods are larger than humans when convenient – for example at the apex of a pediment, but they may come down to a more human scale too – for example Athene with Heracles at Olympia – depending on the format.

To sum up, the Parthenon frieze has directionality and unity. It begins, gathers pace, pauses, and reaches its destination at the east portal of the temple. This is also what worshippers do – and as they reach the main portal, there is a display of gods, both inside and out. Gods fight giants on the metopes, gods are seated on the frieze, the pediment gives us a scene on Olympos, and the open door will reveal the colossal chryselephantine Athene within.

The pediments, 438-432 BC

We are told the subjects of the pediments by Pausanias. This is lucky because what remains is not enough to identify the themes. He says: '... everything on the [east] pediment has to do with the birth of Athene; the far side [west] shows Poseidon quarrelling with Athene over the country'

93

44. The west pediment of the Parthenon: seventeenth-century drawing by
Jacques Carrey. *Above*: left side; *opposite*: right side.

(Pausanias 1.xxiv.5). In each case, the central motif is now missing, while
the extremities are left. The seventeenth-century AD drawing of Jacques
Carrey, and ancient copies of individual figures, show us what the complete west pediment was like (Fig. 44). But the arrangement of the central
motif of the east pediment is still conjectural.

The west pediment, first to be seen by the visitor, had a dynamic
centrepiece with crossing figures, pulling away from each other (Fig. 44).
They are competing to give their name to Athens: probably each creates a
gift – Athene an olive tree, Poseidon a salt-spring. The contestants are
well-balanced, Poseidon appearing dominant while the actual winner is
Athene. These divine figures fill the apex (although what the space between them may have held, whether an olive-tree, a thunderbolt, is
unknown). Behind each god appear their rearing horses, their chariot and
their charioteer. Poseidon's is Amphitrite, his sea-goddess wife: Athene's
may be Nike. Beyond these are smaller figures, thought to be kings and
heroes of Attica, and in the corners are river-gods of Athens. Athene, to
the viewer's left, is backed by King Cecrops with snaky tail and one of his
daughters. Beyond them is thought to be reclining river-god Ilissos, accom-
modating himself to the corner position. To the far right is perhaps the
local spring, Callirhoe. So, as at Olympia, rivers set the geographical
scene. It is Athens, in fact, the Acropolis.

This pediment is particularly crowded. There were about 29 figures in
all. If this was thought desirable by the designers, it should be asked why,
and also what design problems this led to. The scene is a very public one

94

– the contest between two major gods is being judged by the repre-
sentatives of Athens. Clearly for a democratic or valid judgement to be
made, a crowd is required. But a crowd on a pediment needs to read well
from a distance. Here the protagonists take up their own space in a
successful chiastic or 'crossing' pose (so successful in fact that it will
become a 'classic'). The rest of the characters are smaller in scale.

The composition has been criticised for its inconsistency of scale. However, it should be noted that there is a convention, already used on the
Parthenon frieze, that gods are larger. If this is borne in mind, there is no
inconsistency. The lesser deities, heroes, kings and rivers are able comfortably to crowd the further reaches of the pediment, giving the desired effect.
In addition, there is sensitivity in the size-reduction, which respects the
pediment form and even acts as a kind of perspective.

In contrast, the east pediment is peopled entirely by Olympians and the
scale is more consistent (Fig. 45). The problem of the extreme corners is
solved in a completely different way. Beyond the reclining full-size figure
at each end are the horses of Helios and Selene, sun and moon. It is
understood that the pediment floor is the horizon, behind which the
heavenly bodies can rise and set. We see little enough of the two charioteers,
and their horses are represented by the eager heads of one set, the panting

45. The east pediment of the Parthenon, left side (replica).

95

heads of the other. The presence of rising sun and setting moon sets the time of the scene – dawn – on Athene's birthday: they also set the pace – the movement of heavenly bodies is slow. The lazy turn of a goddess's head is the fastest action here. And the heavenly bodies suggest that the scene is set on Olympus.

Athene was born fully-grown from the head of her father Zeus. It is thought that the moment depicted is that just after the birth, not the violent action of Hephaistos as he releases Athene from the head of Zeus with his axe, but a few moments later when the new-born goddess is displayed calmly in her glory beside her father. Zeus will give her the **aegis**, so the power which she wields to make Athens victorious is securely underwritten by the king of the gods. At this moment it is appropriate that Athene is surrounded by her peers. Their presence validates her full godhead which protects Athens.

The stubborn problem with the composition is the vanished central group. Plenty has been written about it. Zeus has been proposed in profile or in three-quarter view in a number of combinations. He may have been a large frontal throned Zeus who would serve as a rehearsal for the colossal Zeus of Olympia: equally he may have been standing centrally between Athene and perhaps Hera, as he stands on the east pediment at Olympia. The principle at stake seems to be that of narrative clarity combined with symmetry and appropriate grandeur. We have already seen how successful a dominant Zeus can be in a pediment.

It will be seen that the preserved figures balance each other visually in a symmetry of opposites – for example the reclining male nude to the viewer's left is balanced by a reclining draped female to the right (Aphrodite). Each side has a close group of three figures, reclining, seated, standing, and so on. For the viewer, there is an endless invitation to compare and contrast, letting the eye rove from side to side, finding more correspondences: clearly this invitation is deliberate and intended.

In both pediments, all figures are carved in the round and are completed on the back almost as much as the front. It seems quite possible that they were put on display on the ground before they were ever raised to the pediments, and would then have been appreciated from all sides. Plutarch reports that: 'The rumour was put about that Pheidias arranged intrigues for Pericles with free-born Athenian women, when they came on the pretext of looking at works of art' (Plutarch, *Life of Pericles* 13). Plutarch gives no credence to the accusation but it must be plausible that respectable Athenians had the interest to visit and inspect the sculpture as such, before it was installed on the temple. When in situ, the over-life-size pieces were stabilised with iron bars fixed in the tympanum at the back and bedded in the stone shelf under the largest statues.

8. The Parthenon

The statue of Athene Parthenos

The sculptural programme was completed by the colossal gold and ivory Athene Parthenos inside the cella.

We have noted earlier that the temple interior was made extra spacious while colonnade space was lost (Fig. 37); this arrangement can only have been for the benefit of the statue. There were also two eastern windows, an unusual feature in a temple, so the interior was deliberately made both light and spacious. These windows would have directed their light down the side aisles, so the entire cella would have been light-filled, with no shadowy areas. In front of the statue was a shallow rectangular marble-lined pool of water. Pausanias tells us this was to counteract the effect of dryness on the statue, which was of course wooden under its coating of ivory and gold. The pool must have increased the available light by reflection, like a mirror. In sunlit or lamplit conditions, one can imagine that wonderful effects of gleaming gold and shimmering ivory would have played all over the cella, and over the statue itself, especially if the water were stirred. It is not known whether this pool was the first of its kind, or was added in response to the dark oily pool made for Pheidias' Zeus at Olympia.

The Athene Parthenos was made by Pheidias, almost certainly before he made his Zeus of Olympia. The chryselephantine technique was already an old one, but the colossal size was quite possibly new; the statue was 11.54 metres in height. The Pheidian style can be guessed at from the figures of the Erechtheion caryatids. Athene would have stood like them, upright with one leg relaxed, in modest feminine draperies, but also with aegis and helmet, shield and spear. In her right hand, she carried a two-metre golden Victory, supported on a pillar. An ancient marble replica gives a general idea of the long-vanished colossus (Fig. 46).

Pausanias describes for us the elaborate iconography of the figure: the golden helmet of the goddess was bristling with griffins and a sphinx. She wore her aegis with a central Gorgon's head in ivory. Her shield sheltered a sacred snake. Three of the themes were already on the temple exterior: on the shield's outer side was carved an Amazonomachy, inside was painted a Gigantomachy, and on her golden sandals was a Centauromachy. A new story was the Creation of Pandora, executed in gold figures on the marble base (Pausanias 1.xxiv.5). Victory (Nike) of course was a major Acropolis motif. This Athene was simply the most glorious of all her many artistic manifestations on or off the Acropolis.

Did the Parthenon serve any practical purpose?

Cults and festivals were an important element in the social cohesion of a polis. The great temple of Athene Parthenos was a visual symbol for the Athenians, gloriously reminding them at all times of their greatness and

97

46. Athene Varvakeion,
an ancient small marble
replica of Athene
Parthenos.

unity. However, it is often pointed out that the Panatheniac worship and
offerings actually centred on the altar of Athene and the image of Athene
Polias, both situated on the north side of the Acropolis; Athene Parthenos
was not a cult-image in the sense that Athene Polias was.

The statue of Athene Parthenos was plated with a great deal of remov-
able gold and it was not thought inappropriate for Athens to 'borrow' this
gold in times of national necessity – so long as it was replaced. Inscriptions
also record the large amounts of gold and silver objects kept in both
chambers of the building, probably for use in rituals. These were secured
not only by great lockable wooden doors, but also by bronze grilles across
the porches.

In Aristophanes' comedy *Lysistrata*, in a bid to put an end to war, the
women barricade themselves into the Acropolis sanctuary; their plan is to
trade sex for peace. It soon becomes clear that by taking possession of the
sanctuary (*Lysistrata* 486-97) they have also gained control of the war-

chest or city exchequer. Where could this have been kept? Some valuable goods, including armour, must have been kept in the Chalkotheke or bronze-store, situated between the Parthenon and the shrine of Artemis Brauronia (Fig. 35). But judging from the large amount of gold and silver objects stored in the temple, it seems that the Parthenon itself may have had a role also as a treasury.

Conclusion

The Parthenon was the first building in Pericles' re-creation of the Acropolis sanctuary. In many ways it is the iconic building of his programme. Its existence is a testament of his vision, which was to ignore expense and to have something built which would fully express the greatness and supremacy of Athens.

The verdict of Plutarch, written in the second century AD, still seems more than valid:

> The buildings went up, as remarkable in sheer size as they were matchless in form and grace, since the workmen strove to excel in the beauty of their workmanship ... For in its beauty, each [building] immediately seemed antique, yet to this day remains in perfect bloom, and fresh, as though brand new (Plutarch, *Life of Pericles* 13).

The Propylaia

Before Pericles

Since late Mycenaean times, there had been a stone-built propylon or fortified gateway on the west side of the Acropolis, the only side that gave moderately easy access. The western slope offered the best approach to peaceful visitors and also most needed defending from attackers.

The Mycenaean propylon would have been something like those still to be seen at Mycenae and Tiryns. It was turned at an angle to the direct ascent, and channelled visitors (or attackers) into a corridor or forecourt before they could arrive at the gate itself. The propylon had formed a defensive unit with the cyclopean wall surrounding the whole Acropolis.

The Cyclopean wall continued as the fortification wall of the Acropolis right up to the Persian sack of the city. The Mycenaean propylon, however, was replaced, shortly after Marathon (490 BC), with a more up-to-date Doric propylon of marble, limestone, stucco and timber. The few die-hards who remained to man the Acropolis against the Persians relied on this gate for protection – identifying it as the 'wooden walls' of the Delphic prophecy. It suffered in the sack along with most of the Cyclopean wall.

A broad approach ramp dated from the expansion of the Panathenaia in 566 BC: a bigger procession would have been enabled by the great ramp of beaten earth whose archaic stone substructure can still be seen under the present access road.

For a yet grander Acropolis, a new gateway was needed. To match the new Parthenon temple, the gateway needed to surpass all others.

The Periclean Propylaia

The Propylaia ('gateways') was the second of the great Periclean Acropolis buildings; the name of the architect, Mnesicles, is known from inscriptions and from literature.

As soon as the Parthenon was finished in 438, work started on the Propylaia and continued until 432 when the pressures of the Peloponnesian War with Sparta became too great for building work to carry on. Whether or not the design was ever fully completed is a moot point which will be discussed below. However, even as it stood, the building was clearly considered an architectural triumph.

The Propylaia went way beyond what was functionally necessary, and clearly was intended to make a grand statement (Fig. 34). From the approach route and from afar, the white marble structure appears toweringly high (Figs 50, 71), and, from below, appears more massive than it really is. This is the result of clever use of topography. The entrance area rises around the approaching visitor like the seating area of a Greek theatre, but, as in a theatre, there is less substance behind it than appears. The real measurements are large, the central section of the building being about 20 metres wide; yet approaching viewers lose all sense of scale as they are gradually enclosed by a total environment of white marble and the outer world is left behind.

Like the Bronze Age propylon, the new Propylaia engulfed the visitor, but there was nothing military about the new building. Fine marble replaced the Cyclopean boulders, columned wings spread out invitingly, a smooth ramp made ascent easy. By-passing the stairway to the Athene Nike shrine on the right (see next section), and looking ahead, the viewer would recognise the familiar form of a Doric 'temple' front with its obligatory three steps (plus one), and the smaller stoas rising up on each side, also with steps. The design appeared symmetrical as was expected in a Greek monumental building, but topography dictated that some sleight-of-hand was needed to get this effect.

The Propylaia is a bewildering building. Even the visitor actually standing in front of it will find it hard to take in more than a general impression. Essentially, the obstacle to comprehension is also the obstacle which Mnesicles the architect brilliantly overcame: the fact that the building has to incorporate many levels and fit an awkward site, while remaining visually impressive.

The vast expensive structure, no longer military, still served the basic purpose of letting people in or keeping them out. In Aristophanes' comedy *Lysistrata* (performed 411 BC), the rebellious women of Athens are supposed to seize the Acropolis and barricade it. So the sanctuary could be easily closed off; the Propylaia was both a physical and a psychological division between the outside world and the sanctuary.

Ground plan and cross-section

Careful study of the ground plan (Fig. 47) will show that the essential core element of the Propylaia is the cross-wall pierced by five lockable doors, graduated in size. To the west of this is a Doric hexastyle prostyle porch linked to the cross-wall by the colonnaded wide corridor; through the doors, to the east, is another similar porch giving onto the Acropolis (Fig. 48). On the west, the building is elaborated in a unique way with wings or small stoas at right angles to the central section. Extra drama is added to the structure by these columned wings, set high up on each side to north and south.

The cross-section drawing (Fig. 49) shows how the ramp rises smoothly between the wings and two paved flanking passages and emerges through

101

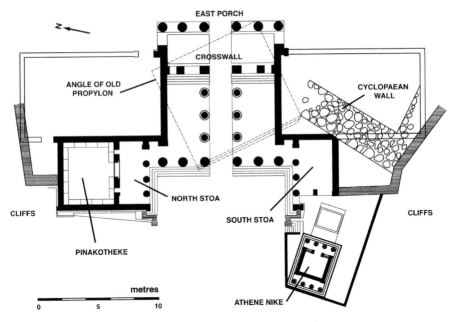

47. Ground plan of the Propylaia including the Nike sanctuary.

48. Reconstruction view of the Parthenon seen through the east porch of the Propylaia (the cross-wall and Ionic columns have been removed for clarity).

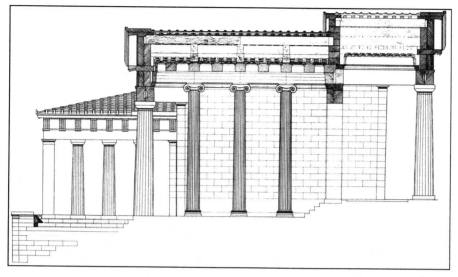

49. Cross-section reconstruction of the Propylaia.

the east porch onto the sanctuary plateau. To reach the same desired level, the paved flanking passages use the four entrance steps on the west and five inner steps on the east.

To accommodate the ascent at roof height, the eastern part of the roof has been stepped up, just at the point of the cross-wall and the five steps.

The central section

As visitors ascended the steep stretch of the Panathenaic Way, they saw the gateway above at a sharp angle. Today, the rock and marble path zig-zags up: originally there was a straight ramp (perhaps stepped on each side). Ahead is a fairly conventional 'temple-style' Doric hexastyle porch, raised on four steps (Fig. 34). The visitor reaching the four entrance steps then enters the building through a shallow porch giving onto a 'corridor' about as wide as the porch. The corridor is divided into three 'aisles' by two rows of three lofty yet slim Ionic columns. The floor of the central aisle is sunk down and is a continuation of the sloping ramp, intended for animal access. The raised side sections are paved with marble and are level for pedestrians.

This 'corridor' ended at the cross-wall with its five graduated doors. The ramp rose smoothly through the large central door. The paved side sections ended in a flight of five steps to reach the two sets of side doors. Beyond the doors, visitors emerged into the east porch at the sanctuary ground-level – which however continues to rise fairly steeply. Ahead, to the right and higher up, is the Parthenon. To the left was Pheidias' twelve-metre bronze Athene Promachos raising her spear. Visitors emerged from shadow into the bright upper air of the sanctuary and were faced with a glittering sacred space – the city having vanished far below. It would have been rather like an ascent to Olympus, home of the gods (Fig. 48).

The north and south wings

The wings were an unusual feature, adding significantly to the impression of size and grandeur. Each wing (Figs 47, 50) is fronted by a three-columned stoa or open colonnade whose floor is continuous with the paved floor of the central building. Each stoa is fronted by four steps, continuous with the four approach steps of the central section: but, as the sloping ramp falls away so sharply, the stoa steps give onto a sheer drop and are purely decorative. The resulting marble 'cliff' on each side is highlighted by a course of dark Eleusinian limestone forming the bottom step of the four. Vertical smooth white ashlar masonry below adds to the impression of Olympian size.

From the approach ramp, the wings appear symmetrical, but behind the identical three-columned Doric stoas they are adapted for different purposes (Fig. 47). The north stoa is slightly shallower and forms the

50. The Propylaia from the west.

entrance porch to a spacious room with off-centre door and two windows. The off-centre door suggests that the room was intended for dining: couches would typically be arranged round the walls of a **symposium** room asymmetrically, and this one could have accommodated seventeen couches. But the room is usually known as the Pinakotheke or Art Gallery because Pausanias describes for us the sizeable collection of important panel-paintings which he saw there, including 'old masters' by Polygnotus. As the room was probably used for entertaining VIPs, impressive decoration would be appropriate.

The design of the south wing (Fig. 53), while appearing symmetrical from the ramp, was modified to provide an easy way into the adjacent sanctuary of Athene Nike. The stoa itself provided shade and rest for visitors after their steep climb. Where the north stoa is completed with the west wall closing off the stoa and the dining room, the south stoa has an open entrance to the Nike sanctuary, and in fact is slightly shortened; this irregularity is visually masked by an anta marking the corner. The roofs of the two wings were **hipped** (i.e. sloping on all sides: see Fig. 34), while the more important central section was pitched and pedimented like a temple.

Ionic spacing

The ground plan (Fig. 47) also shows that on the west and east façades the Doric porch columns are not evenly spaced. The building had to cater for the Panathenaic procession with its 100 sacrificial cattle who had to emerge onto the Acropolis without crowding or jostling, since the calm behaviour of the animals was of importance for the success of the sacrifice. So Mnesicles adopted an Ionic solution: he widened the central intercolumniation, thus creating a more open access (Fig. 51).

An Ionic colonnade can easily vary its spacing in terms of its entablature, since an undivided frieze is extendable. However, with a Doric divided frieze (as here) there could be a problem because triglyphs must be centred above and between columns. Mnesicles found a solution: he increased the gap by one metope and one triglyph, keeping a symmetrical pattern but widening the entrance. The larger gap exactly aligns with the wider central doorway. Ionic influence here asserts itself in a very practical solution to a practical problem.

Decoration

It seems that no sculpture was planned for the Propylaia. Metope carvings would have to have been put in place at an early stage of building, so their absence is clearly intentional. If acroteria were planned they do not seem to have ever been put in place. The Propylaia was left deliberately plain in

51. The Propylaia from the east.

order to offset the abundance of sculpture on the three main Acropolis temples and to differentiate its function.

Despite the general restraint of the design, there are some innovative decorative details. One trend-setting idea is the use of dark limestone strips to contrast with the creamy Pentelic marble. Dark limestone is used for the bottom step of the four wing steps, and also for the top step of the five on the east end of the passage. Linking these dark accents, the corridors have fine large **orthostate** slabs of the same dark stone forming a long dado (emphasising the directionality of the passage). Thus the theme of colour contrast is carried right through the building. (This idea will be used in a more showy way on the Erechtheion.)

The Doric columns are matched in style to those of the Parthenon itself. The Ionic columns, higher and slimmer than the Doric, have plain bases with a double **torus** linked by a **scotia** (Fig. 52). The capitals too are restrained with just an egg-and-dart decoration linking the volutes, and a small honey-suckle in the corners. Possibly these give a clue to the style of the vanished opisthodomus columns in the Parthenon.

Pausanias praised the ceiling of the Propylaia: 'The Propylaia has a ceiling of white marble which in the size and beauty of the stones remains supreme even to my time' (Pausanias 1.xxii.4). Pausanias, usually so unobservant, must have been impressed by the immense length of the marble beams which spanned the corridors, almost six metres each side. The coffering between the beams was painted with colourful patterns and enlivened with gold stars on blue.

Refinements received special attention. The stylobate was not curved –

52. A column base from the Propylaia showing unremoved finishing layer of floor.

probably because the middle section was removed for the central four-metre-wide ramp. But the pediments did curve in the expected way, exactly as on the Parthenon. The Doric columns also matched the Parthenon in tapering, entasis and inward inclination.

Iron beams

Normally Greek architecture is held together by gravity and the accurate fit of the structural elements. A small amount of dowelling and metal clamps is added as a precaution, because of the risk of earthquakes. In the Propylaia, the weight of the six-metre marble beams spanning the corridors from side to side seems to have worried the architect so much that he opted to use some reinforcement. Slim iron rods are imbedded in the tops of the marble architraves of the two Ionic colonnades which support the beams (Fig. 49). They were placed in parallel pairs to take the weight of the marble cross-beams, not above the columns (which already act as supports) but in the gaps between them where intermediate beams rest. The weight of these beams and the ceiling coffers was so great that this reinforcement seemed a good precaution to the architect. It is now thought that the marble structure was in fact sufficient, but this apparent anxiety reminds us of the experimental nature of the building and the daring of the designer at the time.

Propylaia and Parthenon

The Propylaia is on the same axis as the Parthenon, increasing the sense of a 'match' between them. In order to create this alignment, the previous smaller propylon had had to be completely demolished as it had turned more to the south, at an oblique angle to the ascent (Fig. 47). This deliberate change of direction resulted in several superb improvements. The new angle, facing square on to the broad Panathenaic Way, was far more triumphal in effect. From it were seen the sea and Salamis, site of the great victory; directly ahead and clearly visible would have been the defensive Long Walls linking Athens to her harbours on the coast about five kilometres away. In the other direction, the match with the Parthenon, both in angle and in style, resulted in a very grand scheme since the two massive structures now appeared as a unity. The natural topography added to the grandeur since the Parthenon was so much higher up than the Propylaia, and, from a distant view would appear as a higher storey of the already split-level gateway (Fig. 71).

On emerging from the inner doors, viewers were faced with the Parthenon ahead and to their right. This view was the most perfect possible – the three-quarter angle, showing all the features of the architecture at one glance. It was a comfortable distance away, and dramatically higher up. No other view of the temple as an individual structure is quite so good or so impressive (Fig. 48).

In architectural style, the Propylaia matched the Parthenon, with variations. The Doric columns were styled similarly, though in three sizes. The largest were on the west porch, the smallest were on the wings, the east porch columns matched those of the temple, which they face. There was the same mix of Doric with Ionic as in the Parthenon, and for the same reason, namely that Ionic columns could be much higher in proportion to the space needed for their bases.

This planned axial co-ordination between buildings was an innovative and influential idea. By it, the sanctuary itself gained a new kind of unity. In addition, it created a powerful sight line, linking the sanctuary with other significant elements of the polis – its defences and harbours. By this link between harbours and temple, through the gateway, Athene's protection was invoked and her character as victory goddess was proclaimed.

Unfinished work?

There is one mystery about the Propylaia: it appears unfinished. The features commonly cited to prove its unfinished state are these:

- The presence of many **lifting bosses** (small knobs of stone used in the process of construction which were normally removed afterwards), especially on the two flanking walls (Fig. 51).

- Non-removal of the **finishing layer** (extra stone protective surface removed at the last stage) around the columns in the corridor floor (Fig. 52).
- Indications in the stone-work around the flank walls of the east porch that two large rooms (Fig. 47) might have been planned to north and south; i.e. antae and provision for beams.

And yet even after work ceased on the gateway in 432 BC, two more main buildings of extensive workmanship were started and completed on the Acropolis. Since there were plenty of skilled workmen available onsite at a later date, why were they not asked to do the minimal task of removing the bosses and the finishing layer?

Had the two large rooms been constructed as projected by some scholars they would have overlapped the neighbouring shrine of Artemis Brauronia to the south and even risked projecting over the edge of the Acropolis itself. Were such rooms really required, and if built, might they not have overbalanced the whole Propylaia aesthetic by their enormous size? On the western side, the building seems Olympian in scale. This effect is achieved by the use of the natural slope, the addition of wings, the height from city level and (on a clear day) the vast panorama of coast, sea and islands. From within the sanctuary, the eastern porch (as built) looks quite small, dwarfed by the rising ground and the display of wonders within (Fig. 51).

A further point of great interest is the surviving remnant of the Mycenaean wall (Fig. 51, extreme left). This part of the wall once abutted the Mycenaean propylon. Now the eighteen-metre stretch of impressive Cyclopean boulders remains as a memorial to the ancient fortress of Athenian kings. Not only does the ancient masonry touch the Propylaia, but the classical masonry has been cut away or bevelled to allow the venerable wall 'built by giants' to merge with the smooth white ashlar surface of the classical building.

We will later see how the ashlar facing of the Nike bastion is broken open to reveal the rough Cyclopean masonry and bed-rock within: the perfection of the classical masonry is deliberately interrupted to allow the deep past to show through. It may be that the lifting bosses were eventually left on purpose to imply the very opposite of this – the bosses may imply a process which is not over yet; the masons' work is in touch with the future as well as the past. Besides, they have a decorative quality which nicely relieves an expanse of featureless wall (Fig. 51).

The Propylaia, interpreted in this way, would not only mark the transition between the lower city and the sanctuary: it would mark a transition between past, present and future. But above all, it is a glorious building which grants the Athenian citizen a godlike experience and an Olympian approach to the sacred upper city.

The sanctuary of Athene Nike

The temple of Athene Nike – Athene joined with Victory – is the first of all the Acropolis buildings to greet the visitor (Fig. 53). Its platform is located outside the gateway and the remnant of Mycenaean circuit wall; strictly speaking, it is separate from the Acropolis sanctuary (Fig. 34). Considering that 50 years earlier the citadel had been completely sacked, there was amazing bravado in exposing this tiny, exquisite shrine on an eminence, outside any fortified wall. The positioning was itself a claim to complete victory. A sculpted marble balustrade surrounded the platform, whose only practical purpose was to stop visitors toppling off. Sparta famously boasted that her powerful city needed no walls: Athens made her walls into artworks.

53. The temple and buttress of Athene Nike from the west.

10. The sanctuary of Athene Nike

The bastion

In Mycenaean times this rocky outpost of the Acropolis was a natural bastion, projecting out to the right of the propylon, and enhanced with Cyclopean masonry. It could have been additional protection for the gate when the rock was basically a fortress.

By the mid-sixth century BC the old bastion was already being used as a sanctuary for the worship of Athene Nike; the archaic image was probably a seated Athene holding a helmet for protection and a pomegranate for prosperity. During the Persian sack in 480/79, this sacred image was safely evacuated along with Athene Polias. On its return, it seems the image was protected by some kind of simple shelter on the site, for the continuation of worship.

A programme of Acropolis renewal would need to include this shrine, considering the obvious value placed on the image. Equally important was the location: first-fruits for the goddess, first impressions on the visitor. This area had to fit in with the overall Acropolis scheme in design and in excellence. It is also understandable that, as the smallest of the projects, it should be left for completion nearly to the last, especially as it seems it was able to function as a shrine in the interim.

The date and the priestess document

Around 450-445 BC, the same period as the inception of the Parthenon, a decree was passed providing the appointment of a priestess:

> For Athene Nike a priestess who shall be appointed by lot from all Athenian women ... Payment to the priestess shall be 50 drachmai plus the legs and hides from public sacrifices ...

This apparently new office of priestess, chosen by lot from all classes, makes a nice democratic contrast with that of the traditional priestess of Athene Polias who had to be chosen from the Eteoboutadai family of ancient royal descent. Both offices were for life.

The same marble inscription which made provision for a priestess also records that Callicrates was given responsibility for planning the sanctuary. The decree authorises doors to the sanctuary, a temple, and a marble altar 'as Callicrates shall specify ...'. However, at this early date, attention may only have been paid to the temporary shrine, and the structural work needing to be done on the crumbling bastion. Meanwhile the Parthenon and Propylaia were built. Not until 424/3 was a further decree recorded on the same piece of marble, confirming the payment to the priestess; this seems to suggest that the sanctuary is only now in business and the temple finished. The later finish date accords with the style of the architectural sculpture. Also, between the finishing of the Propylaia and the start of the

111

Nike temple, an expensive war with Sparta had begun – the Peloponnesian War. These two events easily explain any delay in starting the project.

Some scholars suggest that the Ionic style of the Nike temple is a result of the Peloponnesian War and indicates that Athens was distancing herself from the Dorian Greeks, now the enemy, and allying herself more obviously with Ionia. This suggestion seems disappointing in that the style of the building could not then be seen as fully part of the Periclean vision, but more as an afterthought. The same would be true of the final temple, the Ionic Erechtheion. The decree shows clearly that the Nike temple was part of the initial thinking; as will be seen later, there are many positive reasons that can be suggested for the Ionic style being intended from the start.

The Nike buttress

Callicrates, in partnership with Ictinos, is recorded as one of the builders of the Parthenon. He was also in charge of building a third Long Wall, joining Athens to the coast – a large engineering work. It is suspected that the talents of Callicrates were more in the area of practical engineering and that the huge and important jobs of preparing foundations and buttressing, planning for the movement of materials, etc., would have been his domain, while the aesthetic features of the Parthenon would have been designed by Ictinos. In this case, there was urgent need for the skills of Callicrates in preparing and renewing the crumbling old Nike buttress and raising its level to fit with the Propylaia.

The sanctuary needed an entrance from the exterior part of the Propylaia, since there was no access from the Acropolis sanctuary. There are actually two entrances – which might suggest a flow of crowds – to avoid a bottleneck. A marble stair, cut into the north face of the buttress, rises from the ramp or main approach to the Propylaia. As the stair reaches the level of the balustrade, the balustrade turns to follow it and a sculptured Nike is seen to climb with the visitor (Fig. 54). (This may have functioned as a pictorial 'Way in' sign.) Visitors can then leave by the false porch of the Propylaia and find themselves back en route at the level of the main entrance hall (Fig. 47). Equally, the level Propylaia entrance must have functioned as a processional route between the two sanctuaries since, at the Panathenaia, the most beautiful cow was selected for Athene Nike and conducted to her shrine.

The new temple replaced an older, simpler shrine consisting at least of an altar and a cult statue protected by a small building. Two blocks from the original statue base were re-used in the foundations of the new altar, demonstrating the importance of continuity in religious sites. Continuity is also found in the buttress itself (Fig. 53). The high mass of bedrock and Mycenaean masonry was squared off with new limestone cladding, resulting in a neat, white, angled buttress, getting narrower towards the front.

112

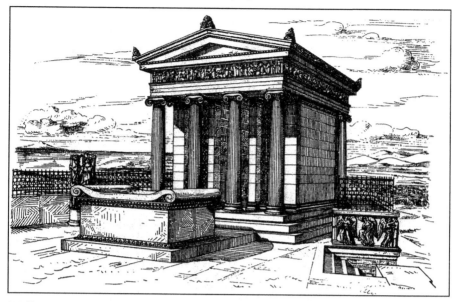

54. Reconstruction drawing of the sanctuary of Athene Nike.

A little above the level of the path, two tall rectangular 'windows' open on the front face, revealing a rough niche in the Mycenaean masonry. This may have been a shrine or shelf for offerings. Round to the north side, where the ramp rises, a polygonal gap is left in the cladding through which the original wall of the buttress can be seen. The contrast of white, **dressed stone** with the Cyclopean boulders and bedrock within is striking. At the foot of the bastion, the limestone blocks splay out slightly at each course; they are left rougher and they are interrupted here and there by the bedrock itself. At the top, the white limestone is finished with a cornice of whiter, smoother Pentelic marble. The bastion, which in effect is a massive plinth for the temple, suggests the spirit of civilisation rising gradually upwards from primitive roots in the earth to the refinement of the Ionic structure above.

The temple

The Ionic **tetrastyle amphiprostyle** temple stands on a neat three-stepped platform abutting the north-western corner of its precinct (Fig. 47), making it as visible as possible from below. It is tiny – 5.4 x 8 metres – with columns four metres high. As with the other Acropolis temples, the first view is of the back (Fig. 53). The Western four-columned porch is purely decorative, containing a blank wall with a plain anta at each corner. The eastern porch (Figs 54, 55) reveals a tiny open cella, once protected by three bronze grilles fixed between the antae and the two plain slim

55. The temple of Athene Nike from the east.

rectangular pillars; this arrangement would have left the statue inside permanently visible. Two more grilles joined the antae to the porch corner columns.

The building is carefully detailed. The Ionic capitals are a half-size version of those in the Propylaia except that the corner volutes protrude at 45 degrees. Linking the rather wide volutes is an egg-and-dart moulding, while tiny honeysuckles fill the angles. The bases have a **reeded** torus above and a rather spreading concave scotia below. The capitals spread very slightly further than the bases. The monolithic shafts are tapered but without entasis. As is typical of Ionic columns, they flare out slightly, very close to the extremities of the rounded flutes. Further details serve to unify the building:

- The reeded moulding and flared scotia of the column bases are mirrored by a moulding at the base of the cella exterior walls, running all round

114

the building. The anta capitals have a simple moulding at the top, similarly carried all around.

- The architrave has the traditional triple-stepped horizontal division: a sharply angled moulding runs along its top, supporting the sculpted ribbon-frieze above. Such details are unobtrusive but they help bind the building together visually.
- The inner porch architrave repeats the triple division. The inner porch rectangular pillars are joined to the side-walls by a strip of the same base-moulding, while the central entrance opening is left clear.
- The lowest course of cella masonry (orthostates) is just over double the height of the courses above: and the upper course height visually relates to the ashlar masonry of the supporting buttress.
- The western façade is finished at the sides with plain dummy antae matching those on the east. All antae are thickened on the flank walls.
- The steps have the typical Ionic groove, undercutting each **riser**. Each riser slopes slightly forward and each **tread** slopes slightly outward.

The designers of this temple had to tackle the problem of visual competition with the adjacent Propylaia. They have adopted various strategies, typical of Acropolis design. The most obvious problem is size. How can a temple the size of a double garage achieve significance when placed next to the majestic Propylaia? One answer (also used by the designer of the Erechtheion), was to go for a contrasting effect, aiming at small and exquisite alongside large, plain and noble. The Ionic style is perfect for the small and exquisite. In fact, the temple of Athene Nike has more than its Ionic share of decoration (Fig. 54), since it seems to have included sculptured pediments as well as the all-round Ionic sculptured frieze which brings interest to otherwise blank side-walls. There were acroteria too. This profusion of sculpture mimics that on the Parthenon itself. In addition, edging the buttress was the unique carved balustrade (which would have faced outward); its wet-look drapery style extends that of the Parthenon pediment yet further (Fig. 56).

To pursue the idea of contrast, the Nike temple is set at a slight angle to the Propylaia (Figs 34, 47). This means that when looked at from the west, the smallest of the temples is distinguished from the others by its angle. The Erechtheion, Parthenon and Propylaia are all set on the same axis as each other.

The Ionic Nike temple borrows the sculpted pediment from the Doric tradition. It has other borrowings too. Tiny as the cella is, its wall thickness tapers on the flank walls, narrowing towards the top like the old mud-brick walls – a Doric feature. This inclination would exaggerate the already sharp perspective of the initial view from below. The slight inward taper of the flank walls is continued in the flank surfaces of the antae. However, the front and back walls and antae do not taper (presumably saving extra work as they are masked by columns).

115

56. Nike adjusting her sandal, a section of the balustrade of the temple of Athene Nike.

The columns at both front and back incline slightly inwards, in the Doric way; and, though slender, they are more stocky than expected for Ionic. They have borrowed a touch of Doric sturdiness from their close neighbour, so as not to appear flimsy by comparison. There is no curvature of the stylobate – this suggests that the need for curvature is a function of size: a tiny temple has no need of a corrective optical illusion.

The sculptural programme

The sculptural programme of the temple links it securely with the Parthenon itself. The pediments, though obviously small, were (it is thought) sculpted with a Gigantomachy to the east, an Amazonomachy to the west. The pairing creates a parallel between Athens and Olympos, a bold comparison already noted on the east and west Parthenon metopes; moving the theme to pedimental level here has made it even more overt.

The marble pedimental figures were attached to the tympanum with pins, suggesting that the tympanum was of a contrasting material, with the white figures creating a cameo effect.

Both pediments were crowned by gilded bronze acroteria – single Nikai at the corners and multiple figures on the apexes, one perhaps incorporating a Bellerophon mounted on Pegasus and slaying the Chimaera. The Nikai perfectly suited the dedication and also echoed the larger golden one carried in the hand of Athene Parthenos, while the hero Bellerophon would provide a picturesque *exemplum* of victory.

The sculptured continuous frieze ran round all four sides of the cella; the precise topics are still under debate. The gods gather on the east, again repeating a Parthenon theme. The battered friezes on the other three sides may show contemporary Athenians at war, as the costumes suggest Greek on Greek and Greek on Persian battles. If so the thematic boldness of the Parthenon frieze is repeated.

The balustrade

The sculpted balustrade was the special glory of the Nike sanctuary (Fig. 54). Rising from the smooth Pentelic cornice which crowns the limestone bastion was a solid marble balustrade, topped with a decorative metal grille of some sort. This barrier would allow visitors to see the view safely – and implies that they were expected to linger and look. The structure surrounded the sanctuary platform on three sides, finishing to the north at the entrance steps, and to the south probably level with the temple front. At the steps, the balustrade turns with them and stops. There were 24 slabs in all, three of which incorporated a corner; two corners were right-angles while the north-west corner fitted the obtuse angle of the platform.

The subject of the carved relief is winged Nikai attendant upon Athene. About 50 Nikai are ranged in varied poses and each side has its own seated Athene. Some Nikai bring arms to build a trophy, marking victory on the battlefield. Others lead bulls to sacrifice. If contemporary Athenian battles really are celebrated on the frieze of the temple just above, this further element of the programme would be an appropriate reference to the fallen, rather like a modern war-memorial. The joyous Nikai raise trophies, while the companionable presence of a seated Athene softens the idea of battle.

In style, this carving has moved a step further than the Parthenon pediments: the flowing drapery is even more body-moulding and deliberately graceful (Fig. 56). Being about one metre in height, the parapet almost duplicates the format of the Parthenon frieze but exceeds it in richness and fluidity. Altogether, the Nike sanctuary with its Doric-influenced Ionic architecture and consciously beautiful sculpture makes a nice foretaste to the main Acropolis sanctuary.

11

The Erechtheion

The Erechtheion, constructed from 421 to 405 BC, was the last, but by no means the least, of the important buildings to be completed on the Acropolis. It is the most unusual architecturally, and in some ways it carried the greatest weight of meaning for the Athenians. As the Acropolis was the religious and historical heart of Athens, so the section of it occupied by the Erechtheion was really the ancient heart of the Acropolis (Figs 34, 35).

The citadel, as we have seen, in late Mycenaean times had a defensible propylon or gate, Cyclopean walls, and, towards the northern edge, a Mycenaean palace, smaller than but similar to those of Mycenae and Tiryns. Visible traces are left of this palace in the terracing which still surrounds the ruins of the 'old temple'.

To the joy of Athenians, this very palace seemed to be mentioned by Homer as the 'strong-built house of Erechtheus' that Athene entered (*Odyssey* 7.81). This mention puts the ancient king firmly back into the age of heroes; archaeologically, it accords with the thinking that Mycenaean palaces included domestic shrines. It also suggests that the patron goddess Athene had dwelt on her hill for a very long time, and was even conceivably present in the ancient palace in the form of the revered wooden statue, Athene Polias.

Myth

While the palace is clearly historical, its famous occupant is rather less so. A kaleidoscope of inconsistent myths cluster about Erechtheus' identity – which on examination seems to merge into other identities, such as Erichthonios and even Poseidon. Poseidon and Erechtheus were worshipped together on one altar in the Erechtheion. The name of Erechtheus is important because it represents just about the earliest 'history' of Athens which could be imagined. The Greeks believed generally that, in earliest times, tribes known as Dorians had swept into mainland Greece and, settling there, had become the mainland Greek nation as they knew it. However, this had not happened in Attica. The Athenians considered themselves to be the aboriginal tribe of their own territory. They had not come from anywhere: they themselves were ancestors of the Ionian group of Greeks who had moved away and colonised the eastern Mediterranean. This Athenian belief in a special relationship with their own soil – known as autochthony – was of extraordinary significance to them and is expressed in the following rather strange myth.

11. The Erechtheion

Athene was hotly pursued by the amorous Hephaistos on the Acropolis. Being a virgin goddess, she rejected him. As she moved smartly out of his way, his seed fell on her leg. She wiped it off with a woollen rag that she then dropped on the ground. But the seed of a god was not wasted and immediately grew up into a child, Erichthonios/Erechtheus. He is frequently illustrated on vases, as Ge, the Earth, waist-deep in earth, hands the new baby up to Athene. Athene had pity on the child and arranged for his upbringing. He became the king and ancestor of the Athenians, and one of his grandchildren was Ion, founder of the Ionian race.

Homer in the *Iliad* – or just possibly an enthusiastic Athenian literary editor of the sixth century BC – seems familiar with the story of Erechtheus and Athene, referring to:

> ... Athens, the well-built citadel
> Nation of great-hearted Erechtheus whom once Athene
> Daughter of Zeus cared for – yet it was the fruitful earth bore him –
> And she set him down in her own rich temple.
>
> Homer, *Iliad* 2.546-9

The myths about Erechtheus and the early kings crowd around this site on the north side of the Acropolis, making the soil itself meaningful and sacred. Cecrops, another of the earliest kings, was buried there, and a sacred snake in an underground crypt was their living representative.

Ion also is a significant character, since he links the ancient royalty of Attica with the Ionian allies of Athens in the Greek struggle to maintain independence against the Persians. During the fifth century, Athens moved on from simple kinship with the Ionians, first becoming their champion, then empire-builder over them; always, the link was of great importance.

Interest in 'roots'

The shrines clustered in the patch of earth just to the north of the 'old temple' were many and all had intimate mythical connections with the beginnings of Athens, her founders, gods and ancient royal family.

Two plays of Euripides, written about this time, suggest that there was quite a ferment of interest in these myths, probably because of the activity on the site and the public expenditure on the new presentation of these treasured cult areas. One play entitled *Erechtheus* deals with the dilemma of the ancient king and his wife Praxitheia who are called upon to sacrifice one of their daughters for the sake of the city. Praxitheia goes on to become the first priestess of Athene Polias, a role still continuing in the fifth century BC, and still an hereditary post of women from the Eteoboutadai family, descendants of the ancient kings. All this ties the royal family and the city goddess together.

Another play by Euripides, *Ion*, tells the story of Creusa, granddaughter of Erechtheus, who was raped by Apollo on the Long Rocks under the Acropolis and there gave birth to Ion, the ancestor of the Ionian race. (This explains a cult of Apollo known as Patroios ('ancestral'), with a temple in the Agora, and a sacred cave in the Long Rocks.) This story too highlights the royal family, its palace, its daughters, and its mythical links with the Ionian race.

These plays of Euripides presented the mythical characters onstage as living suffering people with whom Athenians could fully identify, as they wrestled with the human problems of the rape-victim, the childless couple, the foster-child. Euripides intriguingly helped his audience 'get to know' these ancestors who were also 'neighbours', once dwelling on the familiar rock.

The style

One of the first choices to be made in planning a temple (along with site and material) would be the order – whether Doric, Ionic, or the new 'mix'. The Erechtheion is Ionic and myth may have influenced this choice.

Just for once – in their 'finest hour' – the Greeks as a whole had grouped together successfully, against the Persian foe. But the alliance between 'Dorian' Sparta and 'Ionian' Athens, the two major Greek powers, had definitely cooled by the second half of the fifth century. In fact, they were soon actually at war. It would be understandable if the Doric/Ionic combination of the earliest Periclean buildings yielded to a more insular Ionic. But quite apart from the military and political hostility current at the time of building, it should be no surprise that the Ionic style was chosen for the Erechtheion site with all its time-honoured associations of autochthony and ancestry.

Herodotus – who was himself originally from an Asian/Dorian city, Halicarnassus – generally refers to Athens as Ionian, and tells a little story about this Ionian identity:

> When Cleomenes [King of Sparta] went up to the Acropolis ... he approached Athene's shrine to say a prayer. The priestess [of Athene Polias], rising from her throne, before he could get through the door, cried: 'Spartan stranger, go back. Do not enter the holy place. It is not lawful for Dorians to enter.'
> Herodotus, *Histories* 5.72

This kind of sensitivity makes it possible that the Ionic style of the Erechtheion would have been included in the initial planning of Pericles' carefully balanced programme, and not just as a response to the Peloponnesian War.

The building

The building is so unusual that many points need discussion and explanation. Aesthetically, opinion is divided, some critics viewing it as a triumph while for others it is a product of compromise and incompetence. What is certain is that the quality of workmanship, finish, and elaboration exceeds, if that were possible, the other magnificent buildings already created on the Acropolis. It is also clear that a building was necessary in this area of the sanctuary for Athene Polias, and that some form of monumentalisation was necessary to tidy up the multiplicity of sacred spots and smaller shrines which had long existed there. The Erechtheion was a solution which combined these aims, and which held its own aesthetically in the overall plan of the sanctuary.

The site: what was there before the Erechtheion?

Looking at the ground plan (Fig. 35), it can be seen that adjacent to the Erechtheion on the south is a large area of ruined foundations. As was mentioned in Chapter 7, these are the remains of the 'old temple' of Athene Polias, built in the late sixth century. This temple was aligned with the main altar to its east and therefore was a sensible setting for the Panathenaic sacrifices. The visible foundations show an unusual interior layout, with a double non-communicating cella. While the eastern cella had a double interior colonnade, the western was subdivided into three compartments. This arrangement would be replicated in the new Erechtheion, which suggests that the various cults of that temple were long-standing and revered. It also implies that the Erechtheion is specifically the replacement for the 'old temple'.

The 'old temple' of Athene Polias had been grand for its time. Though it was mainly of limestone, many individual parts of its entablature were island marble. The sculpture was over life-size and was carved free-standing because it was marble whereas the tympanum behind it was of limestone. This temple was badly damaged by the Persians when they sacked the Acropolis in 480/79. The Athenians on their return, having kept the sacred Athene Polias safely with them, must now have housed her either in a remnant of the ruined temple itself, or in some adequate 'temporary' shelter on the site. This situation would have continued from 479 BC until the dedication of the new Erechtheion in 405. The foundations of the 'old temple' are now visible though they may have once been covered over or left open as a memorial to the sacking of the sanctuary by the Persians. Clearly, the temple could have been built up again, just as before. However, this might have been forbidden by the controversial oath of Plataea.

Even without any oath, there were good aesthetic reasons for leaving the old foundations and moving on. Since the Parthenon was to be built as massive as it was, there was little visual space left between it and the 'old temple'. And once the Parthenon had been built, nothing further could be achieved in the line of Doric temples. Also a rebuilding of the now old-fashioned archaic temple would still leave the problem of the adjacent multiple

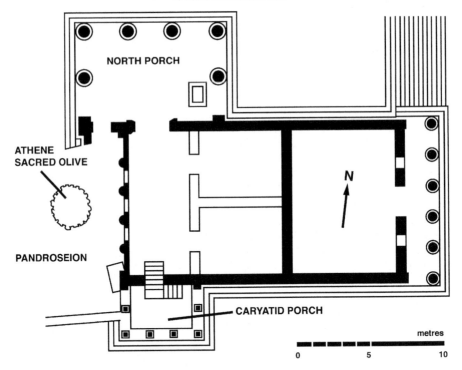

57. Ground plan of the Erechtheion.

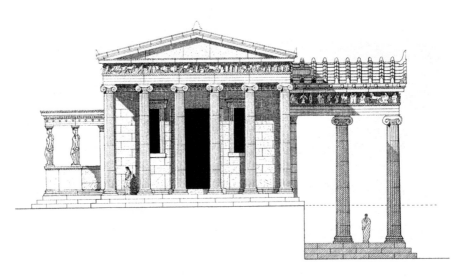

58. Restoration drawing of the east elevation of the Erechtheion.

122

11. The Erechtheion

shrines unsolved, especially now that the aesthetic stakes had been raised so high by the Acropolis team under Pheidias. All significant new building had to reach at least a similar standard of design.

The building

Like all major Acropolis buildings, the Erechtheion (Fig. 57) is constructed of Pentelic marble. It consists basically of a hexastyle prostyle Ionic temple, similar to, but considerably larger than, the temple of Athene Nike. Inside, it has two cellas that were on different levels, east and west. Additionally, it has two very unusual side-porches, north and south (described below). Like the Propylaia, this building has had to be designed on a difficult site in terms of ground-levels, and the designer has solved some unique problems with great ingenuity.

It is often said that the Erechtheion is built on sloping ground, but that is not quite true. The temple straddles an abrupt drop in levels, probably the remains of ancient terracing around the Mycenaean palace (Figs 58, 59). The south and east façades appear to stand on the higher ground (Fig. 60). However, from the north and west, it is clear that the building is double height and has its foundation on the lower ground level (Fig. 61). Outside access to the lower level from the main Acropolis plateau is by a steep flight of steps to the east, and by a roundabout route from the west (Figs 34, 35).

The complex continues on the lower level towards the west with the sanctuary of Pandrosos, once an enclosed garden with an Ionic stoa surrounding it and a tiny temple building. This garden gave access to the

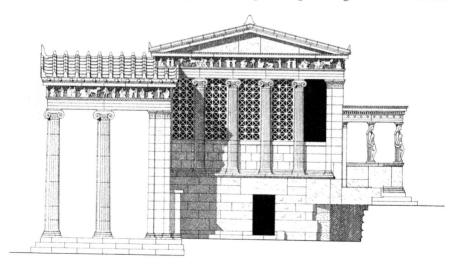

59. Restoration drawing of the west elevation of the Erechtheion.

123

60. The Erechtheion from the south.

61. The Erechtheion from the west, showing the foundation wall of the 'old temple' and the Parthenon.

tomb of Cecrops tucked under the south-west corner of the Erechtheion. It also contained Athene's sacred olive tree and an altar to Zeus Herkeios or 'of the Courtyard' (a feature typically found in Athenian houses) (Fig. 61).

The east porch

The east porch is the most acceptable for those who demand a conventional, symmetrical temple front (Fig. 58). It would have faced the main

124

62. Detail of the entablature from the north porch of the Erechtheion.

altar of Athene and perhaps been the backdrop for the giving of the Panathenaic peplos, since the east cella is thought to have been the new home of Athene Polias. The basic decorative scheme of the temple starts from here and runs all round the building, gathering other features on its way.

The six slender Ionic columns, 6.6 metres in height, stand on a three-stepped platform whose steps are not undercut. They taper elegantly without entasis, as is normal for Ionic columns. However they do lean very slightly towards the cella: a Doric but not Ionic trait. The capitals are very fine with multiple outlines to the volutes; a fine **lotus-and-palmette** ornament running round the neck under the capitals, topped by a tiny beading, an **egg-and-dart** and a small **guilloche** (Figs 4, 62). The corner columns have their corner volutes at a 45-degree angle so that volutes can be seen from both front and flank. This means that the inner side of each corner capital correspondingly has two scrolled sections.

The frieze

The east porch columns supported an Ionic entablature and pediment (Figs 58, 60). The entablature consists of a triple-stepped architrave below a continuous Ionic frieze. The frieze is composed of a dark Eleusis limestone strip as background: to it were once pinned the figures of the frieze, carved separately in white marble to create a cameo effect. Although some figures are preserved, the subject of the frieze is not known; it may perhaps have included myths of the ancient kings. This striking and unusual decoration continued all round the building at the same height – except for a height variation on the north porch.

Both the frieze and the pediment cornices above were outlined by small leaf-and-dart mouldings; they were unobtrusive but gave a neat yet rich finish (cf. Fig. 62). Attention to detail is one of the characteristics of this very expensive building.

The lotus-and-palmette border

The antae inside the east porch have a very beautiful lotus-and-palmette (anthemion) flat capital. This is continued as a border at the same height all round the main cella, with a break only on the west end between the antae. The exquisitely carved anthemion is topped by smaller mouldings, an egg-and dart and a leaf-and-dart, each underlined by much smaller bead-and-reels (Fig. 63).

On the porches, the antae border runs inside the porch, while the architrave and frieze run outside. On the two long flank walls of the temple, the dark limestone frieze, the three-stepped architrave and the anthemion border all run together, piled up in an unusual and very showy ensemble.

63. Mouldings from the Erechtheion. *From top*: leaf-and-dart, bead-and-reel, egg-and-dart, bead-and-reel, lotus-and-palmette (anthemion).

126

Although most of these mouldings are in themselves routine, the effect of piling so many together, and then joining them with the frieze, is a richness that was obviously considered desirable for the purpose. On this temple, the rich mouldings are set off by large expanses of completely featureless marble wall (Fig. 60).

At the feet of the antae is a reeded double torus moulding which also continues all round the building, just above the triple-stepped platform. All these prominent continuous features do much to bind the diverse parts of the building together visually.

The north porch

The north porch has its own surprises (Fig. 64). It was the main entrance to the lower cella. Rather than appear as the mere back door to the basement, it receives extra architectural importance from many features. To begin with, it is built on a scale appropriate for heroes or gods, and is disproportionately large to the building it enters.

Unlike the south porch, it was pedimented and had its own pitched roof, almost like a mini-temple (Figs 58, 59). The reconstruction shows that it would have carried its full complement of antefixes and even acroteria. The columns supported the same three-stepped architrave and the dark limestone frieze on a slightly larger scale to accord with the greater height

64. The north porch of the Erechtheion showing the hole in the pavement.

127

of the building here. As on the east porch, the anthemion border separates from the frieze and runs along the back wall of the porch, connecting the two antae (Fig. 64).

The six Ionic columns stand prostyle, four abreast and one behind on each flank (Fig. 57). They are 7.6 metres in height, and even more ornate than the east porch columns. Like those of the east they have a slight taper, but they also have a nearly imperceptible entasis (borrowed from Doric style). The capitals (Figs 4, 62) are even finer than those on the east, and they were originally enlivened with gilding and paint; coloured glass 'gems' of red and yellow, green and blue were inserted into the 'eyes' of the guilloches. (This colour and glass could still be seen in the eighteenth century AD.) The bases were ornate with another guilloche design on the upper torus, each one very slightly different; these designs echo those on the capitals above (Figs 64, 65).

65. Column base from the Erechtheion: guilloche moulding on top torus; plain scotia and lower torus.

The ceiling of this porch (still intact) was the grandest on the whole Acropolis. Its coffers are triple-stepped and each coffer once contained a central gilded bronze star. Each marble beam dividing the coffers is outlined with an egg-and-dart design, carved instead of just painted as would be more usual.

The door to the cella was bordered with multiple fine mouldings, and spaced rosettes on the broad outer border. The lintel was very ornate with egg-and-dart and an anthemion above, between two scrolls (volutes) decorated with **acanthus**. Like the porch itself, the door was scaled so huge as to be fit for heroes or gods: it was nearly five metres high and very slightly tapered, adding to the impression of size by false perspective. The sides of the porch were defined by prominent antae, linked by the anthemion border. All this grandeur indicates the importance to Athens of the cult objects that lay within.

The porch was itself a sort of shrine, since to the left was a hole in the floor, through which a natural fissure could be seen in the rock (Fig. 64). So sacred was this spot, touched by a god (Zeus' thunderbolt or Poseidon's trident) that a corresponding square hole was left in the roof giving clear access between sky and fissure. Somewhere under the paved floor was a crypt where lived the sacred snake or snakes cared for by the priestess of Athene Polias. (Snakes were a not unusual feature of Greek shrines as they were thought to provide a link with the underworld.) Here in the Erechtheion there was an added significance as the earth-born Erich-thonios was snake-legged, as could be seen on the west pediment of the Parthenon. Athene Parthenos also sheltered a snake within her shield – as Pausanias tells us laconically: '... probably Erichthonios' (1.xxiv.7) (Fig. 46).

An oddity of the porch is that it actually overlaps the cella on the north-west corner, far enough to allow for a small door giving onto the open-air precinct of Pandrosos (Fig. 57). This apparent mistake must have been carefully considered. It would have been so easy to provide a separate door in the precinct wall to enter from outside: but the porch entrance binds the precinct more firmly to the temple.

The west end

The eastern prostyle porch is 'normal', but the western end is 'different' (Figs 59, 61). There is no porch, and the four columns, while matching those of the east in style and nearly in height, are embedded in the western wall on the upper level. The end columns are replaced by two piers: below this at ground level is a solid wall with an unobtrusive entrance to the west cella. It is thought that there were originally bronze grilles between the four upper-storey columns and the left-hand pier, and an open space between the last column and the corner pier on the right. (The west end has been tampered with over time.) A pediment above helped to normalise the west façade and this was very important for the distant panorama of the Acropolis as a whole. Under the pediment ran the dark limestone frieze and the architrave. Only the antae carried the anthemion decoration on the west.

The south porch

The south porch starts from the west corner of the south wall, extending for only a few metres, leaving the rest of the south wall plain (Fig. 60). The porch protrudes southward from the main rectangle with the result that

66. The Caryatid porch of the Erechtheion.

it trespasses onto the visible archaic foundations of the 'old temple', and rests upon their terracing. A small entrance was tucked into the north-east corner of the base, and another led from inside the lower cella.

This porch is a unique feature. It takes the form of a high plinth or platform on which stand six over life-size marble maidens as columns (caryatids) supporting a flat roof with a decorative architrave and cornice (Figs 66, 67). The mouldings vary from those on the rest of the building:

- Just under the feet of the maidens, the platform or plinth is topped by a cornice carved with an egg-and-dart moulding; the torus and three steps treatment continues around the base.
- The maidens are crowned by architectural egg-and-dart crowns in the place of column capitals, mirroring the moulding found under their feet.
- The maidens carry a three-stepped architrave carved with widely spaced rosettes; above them is a continuous frieze of Ionic dentils outlined by tiny egg-and-darts above and below, and topped by a plain protruding cornice.
- Since the porch is not the full height of the building, space is left for the anthemion or lotus-and-palmette decoration to continue uninterrupted, as a unifying feature around the top of the cella wall, under the architrave and the continuous dark limestone frieze.

The six maidens themselves stand prostyle in a row of four, with one more behind each corner one: their positions correspond to those of the columns in the north porch. The maidens are almost identical but have slight variations of drapery and hairstyle. Each rests her weight on the outer leg,

130

11. The Erechtheion

67. Detail of the Caryatid porch of the Erechtheion.

while appearing to begin a forward step with the bent leg. The pose is thus a mixture of static and forward moving. It also divides the left- and right-hand groups by leg position. In their hands, it is thought that they once held **phialai** (shallow offering dishes), possibly designed with lobes like the rosettes above. The sculpture is in the Pheidian style of the Parthenon: a graceful yet solid figure-style and flowing body-moulding drapery. The multiplicity of folds catches the strong sunlight in varied ways, especially because of the left- and right-hand stances, the variety giving an illusion of movement among the figures; they seem to move as the viewer moves.

The maidens are suited to their role as columns by a sturdy upright stance, by a strengthening of the neck area with their flowing locks, by the replacement of what might have been baskets on their heads by the architectural member with egg-and-dart decoration, and by a tendency of the skirt surrounding the straight leg to revert to the fluting of an Ionic column – a visual pun.

We know that caryatids were used in Delphi on two of the finest archaic Ionic treasuries. There may have been archaic caryatids on the Acropolis too: caryatids were a lavish feature of Ionic style.

Vitruvius gives the name caryatid to this type of figure and tells a little history to explain it – the people of Carya collaborated with the Persians in the war so their women became slaves as punishment. However, the

131

ancient term for these figures was simply **korai** – maidens. The archaic caryatids of Delphi obviously predate the Persian War; and to link a story of guilt and treachery with the Erechtheion maidens would seem a sad lapse in appropriateness. These high-classical maidens are sometimes said to replace the many archaic korai or girl statues which once crowded the Acropolis sanctuary but were destroyed by the Persians. However, it is more interesting to look at the specific meaning of the Erechtheion itself.

Given that the shrine of Pandrosos actually adjoins the temple, and that daughters figure so profusely in the various myths about Erechtheus and the other kings, it should surely be no surprise that maidens populate and support the south porch, which covers the 'tomb' of King Cecrops. If the maidens carried phialai in their vanished hands, they were equally able to make offerings at the ancestral tomb or to Athene Polias. There is also something about this unique loggia or viewing porch suggestive of the balcony of a palatial dwelling house. One could imagine that from its vantage point, the priestess with her young girl attendants might watch over crowds and ceremonies; alongside them would be the priest of Poseidon (who also had to be a member of the Eteoboutadai family); for onlookers from below, living figures on the porch would move among stone maidens in an intriguing way. Both priest and priestess of the double temple, being descendants of ancient king/priests, were a visible bloodlink with the past.

To the west of the complex was probably situated the House of the Arrhephoroi where girl and women weavers (creators of the ceremonial peplos) were housed. So the maiden theme would continue along the whole north side of the rock (Fig. 34).

Rather similar columnar maidens are found on the Parthenon, on the important east frieze (Fig. 42). Their sedate and maidenly profile-walk on the frieze is replicated by the profile view of the porch maidens, who seem about to join the Panathenaic procession with ready hand-held offerings and forward-leaning pose (Fig. 67). The slow and eternal advance of the Erechtheion korai across the sacred space between the two temples can be seen as linking the Erechtheion with the Parthenon in one unified act of worship to Athene. Cleverly, the frontal view of the Erechtheion maidens is more dominated by the upright weight-bearing leg with its column-like flutings, whereas the more dynamic side-view suggests a forward movement, uniting the two Athene temples across the ruins of a third.

Inside the temple

Internally the temple is split-level and had a double cella (Fig. 57). The eastern section was probably single-storey height (entered only from the east), and the west double-storey. There was no internal access between the two levels. The eastern cella interior floor seems to have been infilled to the upper level height, while the separate western cella floor was on the

132

lower ground level. The western cella seems to have imitated the unusual triple layout of the 'old temple' western cella, while the eastern one replaced the old eastern cella, both still observable from the ruins. However, the exact internal arrangements of the Erechtheion are still debated as subsequent use of the building has destroyed most of the evidence.

Inside the building, there was quite a lot to take in, according to Pausanias:

> As you go in there are altars: Poseidon's, where they also sacrifice to Erechtheus ... and one for the hero Boutes, and a third for Hephaistos. On the walls are paintings of the Boutadai family, and, the building being double, some sea-water inside a well. This is not so very surprising ... But the extraordinary thing about this well is that when the wind blows south it makes a sound of waves. The mark of a trident is in the rock. They say that these things appeared as evidence for Poseidon in his struggle for the land (Pausanias 1.xxvi.5).

Most importantly there was the image of the city goddess – Athene Polias: 'Rumour says it fell from heaven. I shall not go into whether this is so or not' (Pausanias 1.xxvi.6). The heavenly origin suggests that the statue could have been aniconic (non-representational). There were extremely ancient statues of stone or wood of this type, and the antiquity only increased the sacredness. It was this statue which received the gift of a new peplos or dress at every Panathenaia; most likely it was kept in the eastern cella, but this is not certain. The decorative peplos, woven by specially selected women and girls each year, always featured the Battle of Gods and Giants in which Athene had distinguished herself. There is discussion about how these textile works of art could have been displayed and stored: one suggestion is that the long plain stretch of south exterior wall next to the caryatids might have been used as a display area.

Athene Polias was lit by a wonderful golden lamp made by Callimachos which could burn for a year without refilling: 'above the lamp a bronze palm-tree goes up to the roof and draws up the smoke' (Pausanias 1.xxvi.7). There was also an amazing collection of ancient art and contemporary memorabilia:

> A wooden Hermes, said to be the offering of Cecrops, hidden by myrtle branches
> A folding stool made by Daidalos
> Among the Persian spoils, the breastplate of Masistios, commander of cavalry at Plataea
> A Persian sword, said to have belonged to Mardonios. I know Maisistios was killed by the Athenian cavalry, but as Mardonios fought against Spartans and fell to a Spartan, the Athenians could hardly have obtained the sword then, and the Spartans would surely not have let them have it (Pausanias 1.xxvii.1)

Pausanias shows an unaccustomed analytical streak here as he thinks about the authenticity of the Persian spoils. But, as usual, he makes no mention of the architecture.

Was the building a triumph or a disaster?

Each viewer must give his or her own answer to this question.

The temple has been greatly criticised for its eccentric and almost haphazard design. But it should be pointed out that each aspect works well in itself and not all aspects can be seen at once. From east and south it appears a one-storey building. The north porch is impressive from close up, and from afar its height gives it a needed importance. The west view is harder to assess since it was once enclosed and bounded by the garden shrine of Pandrosos. Here too grew Athene's sacred olive tree whose twentieth-century replacement now masks the lower part of this façade. However, from a distance, the west columns and pediment took their place satisfactorily in the general Acropolis line-up of large Doric and small Ionic temple fronts (Fig. 71).

It may be that hostile criticism is simply based on expectation: this temple is different. However, while some scholars may hate it, architects have loved it – as a treasury of ideas. Ancient Greeks, who delighted to reduce anything and everything to component parts and then adore the perfect relation of the parts to the whole, may have found it refreshing to contemplate this eccentric but fresh assembly of perfect elements.

12

The Hephaisteion

The temple and precinct of Hephaistos stand on the small hill bounding the north-west side of the Athenian Agora (Fig. 72). The plan of the temple and the arrangement of the sculpture decoration are designed to give special emphasis to the east front, unlike the Acropolis buildings, which cater for all-round views. The modern path winds upward from the Agora, allowing the visitor both frontal and three-quarter views of the temple, as intended (Fig. 68).

Natural foliage makes the precinct a pleasant place to be. Round three sides of the temple, square sunken pots have been found, once planted with alternating pomegranate and myrtle bushes, an arrangement dating from the third century BC when formal landscaping became fashionable (Fig. 69).

It appears that no sanctuary existed here before the Hephaisteion, so building on this spot would have been no violation of the oath of Plataea. The purpose of the temple was to honour Hephaistos, god of armourers, for his help in defeating the Persians. Since metalworkers were not at the top of the social ladder, this thank-offering was also a nice democratic touch, acknowledging what the working **demos** (people) contributed to the city.

68. The east front of the Hephaisteion

The temple was started in 449 but not finished until around 420, the cult-statues being dedicated 420-415. It looks as though the commencement of the Hephaisteion was among the first architectural signs of confidence and recovery after the Persian War. Around this time, other improvements were being made to the city, both practical and pleasurable; the massive south wall of the Acropolis was built up, paid for by profits from the victories of Cimon, a successful general and a political rival of Pericles. Cimon himself paid for the construction of the defensive Long Walls running from Athens to her coastal port, Peiraeus; and he irrigated the sacred grove of the Academy, and had the Agora planted with plane trees to bring shade and refreshment to the civic space. But Cimon died in 449 and it is not known who promoted the new temple overlooking the Agora. In 447, it was Pericles who proposed the Acropolis renovation. Understandably, the Acropolis now took precedence in using resources, since it was the major city sanctuary, but it was also Pericles' own vision. This explains the long time taken to complete the Hephaisteion.

The building

The Hephaisteion appears to be a standard classical Doric temple, although by now we should not really think that a standard form actually exists.

The building today still retains all its colonnades, the outer metope frieze (though damaged), both inner-porch friezes, and the pronaos (front-porch) ceiling with its marble coffering (Fig. 68). A medieval barrel-vault replaces the ancient terracotta roof and wooden coffered ceiling over the cella. (This was added when the temple was used as a church.)

The temple stands on the usual three-stepped platform, but the lowest step is limestone, which now has the unfortunate effect of blending too well with the ground and visually reducing the height. It is hexastyle with a distyle in antis porch at each end; the flank columns follow the 'formula' of 6 x 2 + 1. The outer measurement is 13.7 x 31.7 metres. Inside is a single cella, with one entrance on the east front (although an entrance was later cut into the back wall). It seems that the foundations indicate a change of plan during construction. The original intention was for a more archaic layout – longer and narrower, but the proportion was changed, early on in construction, to the new classical 'look' as seen at Olympia.

The temple is criticised for having a top-heavy entablature carried on rather slender columns. However this proportion works well from below – the angle from which it is mostly seen – whether from the Agora or from the steep approach path. The architect must have carefully weighed up the advantages of an optical correction which only worked well from a limited viewpoint.

The porches are not equal in size. The ground plan (Fig. 69) shows that the east front porch is deeper than the rear porch: the front antae are set further back than usual, level with the third flank column, and the inner porch is deeper too, bringing the actual cella entrance back to the fifth flank column – a whole columniation further back than the rear porch, where the cella wall is level with the fourth flank column, and the antae are just past the second flank column.

What was gained by all this juggling of proportions? The viewer is most likely to see the temple almost frontally, as said before. The spacious east porch and deeper inner porch offer interesting depths and shadows. Ionic influence, which so often heightens attention to the entrance, can be seen at work here, creating a sense of arrival and of mysterious inner space: yet this has been achieved entirely by Doric methods.

Ionic features

The Doric Hephaisteion adopts some overtly Ionic features, which seem deliberately to quote the ruined Acropolis buildings. Like the ruined Marathon temple, it is all marble (an Ionic feature), except for the lowest

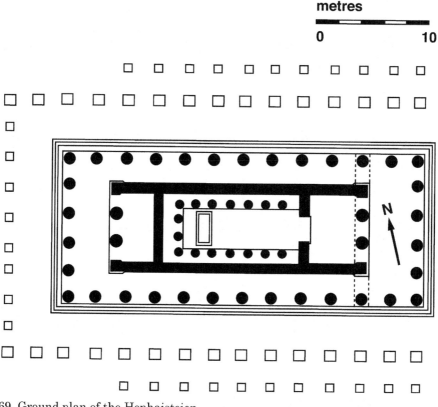

metres

0   10

69. Ground plan of the Hephaisteion.

step. An Ionic moulding at the foot of the cella wall was also a quotation from the ruined Marathon temple.

The Hephaisteion has inner porch Ionic friezes. The 'old Athene temple' on the Acropolis, which was Doric, also probably mixed the orders in this way.

This sequence suggests that the Parthenon itself with its Ionic frieze was following a peculiarly Athenian tradition of mix-and-match, rather than being a surprising innovation.

Innovations

It is questioned whether the Parthenon influenced the Hephaisteion, or vice versa. The Hephaisteion's Ionic frieze could have been added in imitation of the Parthenon, however, the unusual alignment of the east porch antae with the third flank column could not. This alignment – not found on the Parthenon – adds to the emphasis and interest of the front porch because it enables the frieze to stretch from side to side of the colonnade, creating a rectangular 'box', surrounded by sculpture: outside on the front and sides, inside at the back (Figs 68, 69). Sounion, one of a group of contemporary Attic temples, had a rather similar arrangement of a carved Ionic frieze which actually went all round the interior of the front porch, forming a more complete 'sculpture box'. However, in the Hephaisteion back porch, the Ionic frieze runs only from anta to anta and the columns are (as was more usual) not aligned.

All the sculptures of the Hephaisteion are of Parian marble – unlike those of the Parthenon which are of Pentelic. Because the Parian had to be imported, it seems likely that all the marble was ordered prior to construction; the metopes were carved early on in the process as they had to be; but by the time the friezes were carved from the ready-prepared Parian pieces, cheaper 'home-grown' Pentelic had become standard for Athens.

The metopes

The east front metopes are all carved, and so are the first four on each flank, starting from the east corners (Fig. 68). This emphasises the east façade and the approach area.

The carved metopes of the front façade and side angles had to be placed in position during the construction of the colonnade since this was normal practice. The 'severe' style of the carving agrees with a mid-century date and is stylistically comparable with that of Olympia.

The metopes are shared between Theseus and Heracles. (In fact the temple has traditionally been misidentified as the Theseum because of the Theseus metopes, but the real Theseum is now known to have been elsewhere.) These two heroes have shared an Athenian building before –

the controversial Treasury at Delphi. The pair go well together: buddies, action heroes, monster-busters and friends of the down-trodden. Heracles is arranged across the front, Theseus, less divine but more Athenian, has the first four slots down each flank. Heracles takes precedence although Theseus had a special prominence in Athens at this period: his gigantic bones had been recently brought 'home' to Athens by Cimon who had the good luck to 'discover' them while on military campaign in Skyros.

There are no carved metopes on the west façade; this fact points the viewer's attention back to the east front.

The Ionic friezes

The inner porch Ionic friezes seem to have been added after a break of some years; the style is now soft, flowing and Parthenon-like. The east porch frieze shows a battle in the presence of six Olympians. These gods sit in two symmetrical groups of three, framing the inner scene of warriors which they watch, as on the Siphnian frieze – but arranged as on the Parthenon frieze. The west porch has a Centauromachy which also could imply the presence of Theseus. Both pediments contained sculpture and there exist some fine Parian fragments, but not enough for the subjects to be identified.

The internal colonnade

The initial plan for the modestly-sized cella interior was for a simple room with fresco decoration on plastered walls. Some scholars believe that, inspired by the Parthenon, a double Doric colonnade was added for which there was really very little space (Fig. 70). The columns would have returned behind the statues, as in the Parthenon, in a row of three or more. Those on the sides would have been so close to the walls that they would have appeared more like a series of niches than a free-standing colonnade. In fact, it is not certain whether this rather problematic colonnade actually existed at all.

The cult statues

The cult statues (421-415) were joint offerings to Hephaistos and Athene in bronze by the sculptor Alcamenes. Bronze was more normally used for outdoor sculpture: its use here is a direct reference to the special domain of the smith god.

Fig. 70 shows a reconstruction of the cult statues in their setting. Athene is her tall gracious self with helmet and aegis: Hephaistos wears a workman's cap and workman's short tunic: he looks very much as Homer presents him in Book 18 of the *Iliad* where we see him in his workshop. Valerius Maximus (first century AD) tells us that 'the god's lameness was

70. Reconstruction of the interior of the Hephaisteion with cult statues of Athene and Hephaistos.

masked; he stands there displaying some trace of it unobtrusively beneath his garment ...'. To present a god in this down-to-earth way indicates a compliment to the artisans of Athens and a cheer for the democracy which played so great a part in winning the war.

These two gods have special value for the Athenians. Hephaistos (who made the armour of Achilles) is the metalworking god or smith. Around this temple has been excavated plenty of evidence that this was the metalworkers' quarter where armour would have been produced. Clearly Hephaistos needed a special thank-you from the Athenians for his help in defeating the Persians. Athene belongs here too – because she is everywhere in Athens, because she is the goddess of military strategy, and of Victory; also because she too is a craftsperson, patroness particularly of potters and weavers. Appropriately, the potters' quarter (Kerameikos) was behind the temple, adjacent to the armourers'. She is also the 'not really' consort of Hephaistos; he sits next to her on the Parthenon east frieze; he helps release her from the head of Zeus on the east pediment; he collaborates with her (as fellow craftsperson) at the Birth of Pandora on the pedestal of the Parthenos. As the metal-working god, Hephaistos is responsible for the success of the bronze sculpture by which gods (including himself) are revealed.

The two cult statues shared one large base of black Eleusinian limestone, still to be seen in situ. This was probably decorated with white marble or gilded relief figures dowelled on, just as on the Erechtheum frieze; dowel holes can still be seen.

It will be remembered that Hephaistos and Athene were the parents – although unconventionally – of Erechtheus/Ericthonius. The narrative frieze on the base is thought to have shown, not the conception, but the birth of the autochthonous child.

Conclusion

It is often said that the reputation of the comparatively small temple of Hephaistos suffers from its proximity to the glories of the Acropolis. However, it should not be seen as a rival but as a complementary sanctuary. Together, the two sanctuaries sandwich the vital areas of civic and social activity in Athens.

13

Views and their meanings: the Acropolis and its surroundings

The view from the west

The view from the west (Fig. 71) is the only one from which the entire Acropolis line-up fully makes visual sense. From every angle, something interesting can be seen rising over the Acropolis rim even today; in the pristine state of the buildings, there would have been so much more. But only from the west do the buildings range themselves into a single unified composition. Not only do the four major façades (though architecturally the backs) appear from their individual best angle, but also, from a distant and level point west, all the buildings fall into a perfect relationship with each other. Even the somewhat questionable west view of the Erechtheum now makes sense. It 'reads' as three linked entities, the central part with columns and pediment appearing as a quite conventional temple above a precinct wall. The Parthenon is revealed as the glorious crown of the hill,

71. The Acropolis from the Pnyx.

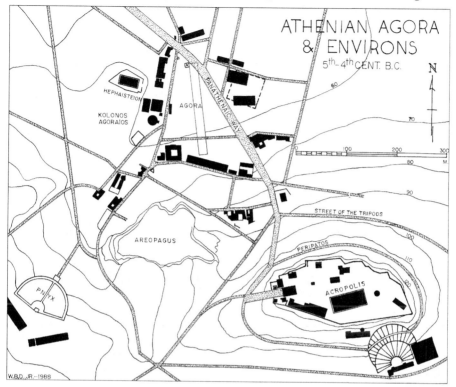

72. The Acropolis and its environs.

being by far the largest and highest up. The Nike below it closes the view; by inclining to the left, it pulls attention back to the centre. There the Propylaia, even at a distance, opens its powerful wings and repeats, on the lower level, the great theme of the Parthenon Doric front. Also central and clearly visible would have been the twinkling spear of the thirteen-metre bronze Athene Promachos (see Fig. 34).

What is this high western viewpoint from which the whole line-up makes sense? It is the Pnyx (Fig. 72), the designated meeting place for the full Assembly of Athenian citizens and the most obvious symbol of the democracy – under which Athens had repulsed the invader Persia and her own old tyrant, Hippias. Whether the speakers faced the Acropolis, or whether the assembled citizen body faced the Acropolis (as each did at different phases) hardly mattered. What was important was the visual link between the two civic spaces, one housing the most democratic process of the city and the other the worship of the goddess, symbol, protectress and patroness of the city. The sense of visual satisfaction derived from the view underlines the purposefulness of this connection.

Looking west from the Acropolis

The westward view may be obtained either from the crowded Propylaea, or more conveniently from the western Nike buttress. Leaning on the Nike balustrade, the ancient viewer had a splendid view of the Pnyx; much closer at hand he would see the Areopagus; and in the distance, the sea and Salamis.

All of these are linked in the history and symbolism of Athenian victory. The significance of the Pnyx is as the gathering place of the demos. The strange reddish rock to the right, the Hill of Ares (Areopagos), was said to be the site of the Amazons' encampment when, in the heroic age, they besieged and attacked the Acropolis, and were beaten back by Theseus. This victory is commemorated on the Nike pediment just at the back of the viewer who is looking west, and will be seen again on the west metopes of the Parthenon and on the shield of Athene Parthenos. All three times it will be paired with the Battle of Gods and Giants. Emphatically, attacks on Athens and on Olympus are paralleled.

Although it was King Theseus who defeated the Amazons, democracy still is in the picture, because Theseus is credited with founding Athenian democracy (see p. 35). The mythology has its important fifth-century parallel. The real-life Persians also encamped upon the Areopagos in 480/79 BC and from it attacked and sacked the Acropolis; ultimately they were defeated by (in the Athenian view) the Athenian democracy. Apart from Marathon, the most defining contribution to Athenian victory was the sea-battle of Salamis, the site of which can be clearly seen from the Nike bastion. Ironically, the evacuated Athenians from their refuge on the island of Salamis could have actually seen the fires of their burning Acropolis: now, on that once desecrated site, pointedly and proudly rose the new monuments of victory. No wonder the Nike balustrade was carved with the most seductive, luxuriant series of 50-odd Nikai, honouring the dead, the victors, and their patroness Athene Nike.

There are further links between the Pnyx, democracy, victory and the Parthenon. The west pediment of the Parthenon (Fig. 44) shows the contest between Athene and Poseidon for patronage of Athens. The two great central gods were flanked by rearing horses. As the pediment narrows, many smaller figures crowd in, both male and female. Those figures – who are ancient kings, heroes, princesses, local nymphs and rivers – are all there to represent Athens – they are there to vote. They choose Athene, and who could argue with that choice? The voters showed their wisdom in picking a victory-bringing patroness, and so give strong encouragement to the citizen body of the fifth century to exercise their right and duty of voting.

But there is also Poseidon. Two major gods, Athene and Poseidon, form the centrepiece of the pediment in their full creative power and as divine antagonists. The clash of gods makes an exciting pediment. It may be

144

objected that it is odd to show a god as the loser as well as a goddess as the victor. However, we need not think of Poseidon as a loser: he will receive worship in the Erechtheum where he had his priest alongside the priestess of Athene Polias. It is true that he will not give his name to Athens – but on the pediment, his magnificent nude musculature is, if anything, more prominent than the slender draped figure of Athene; he is taller and more bulky, and his stretched leg overlaps that of Athene up to the knee (Fig. 44). The traditional superiority of male against female is visually maintained, but more particularly, the balance of sea-power against land-power is asserted. It was by sea that the Athenians were victorious in the Persian wars: Athens owes victory to Poseidon as well as to the warrior Athene. Facing west to Salamis, it is clear that the city cannot do without him. By this sculpture he receives honour and so does democracy – because Athenian democracy and sea-power go hand-in-hand since the navy was manned by citizen oarsmen.

This is reading the Parthenon pediment according to the victory theme; but the gifts of Athene and Poseidon have equal relevance to peace. The benefits of Athene's olive tree are clear: the olive was an essential commodity in the ancient world as its oil was used for lighting, cooking and washing. Yet Athens was absolutely dependent for prosperity on her foreign trade, and this was of course carried on by sea. Athenian pots of Athenian oil and wine went all over the known world to be exchanged for other goods which, with her limited soil and climate, she could not produce. This peacetime collaboration of land and sea further explains the conjunction of deities on the pediment.

Looking south from the Acropolis

From the south wall, the viewer could look down on a range of shrines and sanctuaries. The most important was the sanctuary, temple and theatre of Dionysus (Fig. 72). Here the major drama festivals were staged with their attendant processions and civic ceremonies. Next to it was the Odeion, the covered concert-hall built by Pericles. And clustered in the cliffs of the Acropolis rock itself were various shrines.

If the awakening male nude to the left of the east Parthenon pediment is Dionysus (Fig. 45), as usually interpreted, then he is looking over to his own theatre-sanctuary. If, however, as some suggest, he was actually Heracles, then *he* would be looking at his own shrine of Kynos Arges, also to be found a short distance from the wall.

The view from the south

The southern Acropolis wall was particularly well built up with smooth vertical masonry. From the theatre, the corner of the Parthenon could have been seen rearing up above it, unmistakably. That glimpse of

145

Athene's temple underlined many a political point made on stage; wherever a stage-city was set, the real Athens was never far from the dramatist's mind, or the audience's; for example when Antigone unknowingly sees distant Athens which will be the salvation of her father Oedipus, the actor would surely gesture towards the citadel:

> Father, miserable Oedipus, the towers that crown
> The city, so far as I can see, are still far off ...
> Sophocles, *Oedipus at Colonus* 14-17

Looking east from the Acropolis

The Acropolis plateau rises gradually towards the east. From its furthest point, the drop is dramatic, the view mountainous. From right in front of the Parthenon temple, rocky peaks can be seen to lift above the parapet, but otherwise, the world beyond the Acropolis is cut off, and this area would have been strictly an abode of gods only. In fact it contained other sacred areas, perhaps without buildings, such as that of Zeus Polieus, protector of the city. This is reflected in the god-focussed east front, where only gods are celebrated – except on the frieze where the Athenians bring their offerings in solemn procession, reflecting real-life ritual.

The view from the east

The eastern view of a temple should be the principal one, architecturally speaking. But because of the rising ground, nothing can be seen from below at this point but precipitous cliffs.

It was these cliffs, thought impregnable, which enterprising Persians scaled during the siege of the Acropolis in 480/79. In the natural rock, below the vertical buttressing, there is a large cave sacred to Aglauros, one of the daughters of Erechtheus, linking the east cliff with the main family sites on the North. Pausanias tells us of further events in the life of Erichthonios when:

> ... Athene put Erichthonios into a chest and gave him to Aglauros and her sisters Herse and Pandrosos, ordering them not to meddle with the [contents]. Pandrosos was obedient, but the other two opened the chest, saw Erichthonios [who was snake-legged] and went raving mad; they threw themselves from the sheer cliff of the Acropolis (Pausanias 1.xviii.2).

This east cliff would have been the site of their suicide. (Obedient Pandrosos had her shrine next to the Erechtheum.) In a variant story, Aglauros willingly sacrificed herself, leaping to save Athens, so her sacred cave would have inspired the ephebes, the young trainee warriors, whose base was situated nearby.

146

13. Views and their meanings: the Acropolis and its surroundings

The north cliff of the Acropolis

In the north Acropolis cliff-face are found other impressive caves including the Long Rocks, scene of Apollo's rape of Creusa, and sacred to him.

Also somewhere on this side of the Acropolis is the site of a mysterious ceremony recorded by Pausanias which was carried out annually by women and girls responsible for the weaving of the ceremonial peplos. The House of the Arrhephoroi was on the summit of the north cliff, and below it was the remnant of a Mycenaean well-shaft, traversed by dangerous steps. ('Arrhephoroi' means 'carriers of secret items'.) Pausanias records the ceremony like this:

> Two young girls dwell near the temple of Athene Polias – the Athenians call them Arrhephoroi; these girls live for a season next to the goddess, and when the festival comes round they perform ceremonies during the night as follows. They place on their heads what Athene's priestess gives them to carry, and neither she who gives it nor they who carry it know what it is. Within the city not far off is a precinct called Aphrodite in the Gardens containing a natural underground passage; this is where the girls go down. At the bottom, they leave what they were carrying, and they pick up something else and bring it back covered up. They are then sent away and other girls are brought to the Acropolis instead of them (Pausanias 1.xxvii.4).

This is the finale of the yearly cycle: the mysterious things carried recall the myth of Athene's care for the earth-born baby, Erichthonios, entrusted long ago to the royal princesses.

Looking north from the Acropolis

From the north side of the Acropolis (Fig. 72) the viewer could survey the Agora and the broad processional route linking the Acropolis to the city wall and Sacred Gate, starting-point of the Panathenaic procession. From the gate the Panathenaic route crosses the Agora, passes the Eleusinion (a city outpost of the Eleusis sanctuary) and finally winds up between the Areopagus and the Acropolis till it reaches the foot of the straight ramp leading to the Propylaia.

The Sacred Gate and the adjacent Dipylon Gate lead out of the city, through the Kerameikos burial area just outside the walls, to Eleusis on the coast where the famous mystery cult was celebrated. Between the gates, a large fourth-century building, the Pompeion, housed the equipment and practical preparations for the Panathenaic procession. Here and in the Agora, many of the festival-related activities took place, such as feasting and competions.

73. The north wall of the Acropolis showing column drums (left) and triglyphs (right).

The view of the ramparts from the north

From the Agora, the view of the Acropolis is particularly intriguing. It was an important view since it was in the Agora that the daily public life of the city – social, commercial, legal and governmental – was largely lived.

From this angle it is architecturally very satisfactory that the north porch of the Erechtheion is scaled so large – it shows up well above the ramparts, almost as a temple front in its own right (Fig. 73).

In the north wall under the Erechtheion, the rebuilt rampart incorporates architectural pieces salvaged from the Persian sack, arranged in a deliberate 'architectural' order. To the left, looking up, are unfluted column drums; to the right and higher up the cliff, is a short stretch of triglyph frieze. The column drums must come from the partly-built Marathon temple – they are unfinished. The triglyphs are from the 'old Athene temple'.

This display of ruined elements was inserted into the north wall at some time after the Persian sack of 480/79. It is usually interpreted in the spirit of the oath of Plataea: 'I will not rebuild ...'. But by the time the Acropolis had risen in greater beauty from the ashes, these fragments take on a more triumphant note. They can be read as a layer of history. Like the Mycenaean masonry and shrines visible under the bastion of Athene Nike, they speak of the past; and they carry the more glorious future aloft. In a sense, by crowning the mass of the rock itself with a suggestion of

148

architectural form, columns topped by triglyphs as they would be on a temple, they convert the whole of the rock to a kind of 'natural temple' – above which the new glory of Athens can rise yet higher.

Furthermore, this is the sacred earth from which was born Erichthonius/Erechtheus, ancestor of the race, and where his sacred snake still lived. This precious ground is full of mysteries, at which the triglyph wall hints.

All this mystical history makes it very appropriate that there is also a clear sight-line across the Agora between the Erechtheion and the Hephaisteion (Fig. 72). Hephaistos, who also receives worship in the Erechtheion, is honoured together with Athene in his own temple. We have seen that there is reference to Erichthonius under the bronze cult-statues of his quasi-parents in the Hephaisteion. One may stand in the porch of Hephaistos' temple, looking out at the very spot on the Acropolis which originated the autochthonous race of Athens. The resulting sight-line across the Agora neatly embraces the city, linking the house of the sturdy worker-god with the Acropolis and its more aristocratic associations.

14

The sanctuary of Apollo Epikourios at Bassae

High on its lonely ridge in the snowy mountains of Arcadia, the sanctuary of Apollo Epikourios at Bassae holds a special fascination for many (see map on p. xii). Once striking in its landscape setting (Fig. 74), today the temple can be seen only under a permanent covering or tent, which increases the gloom of its natural dark colouring. The restored structure now stands alone, although the foundations of other sanctuary buildings can be seen scattering the hillside nearby. The almost complete frieze and some other small sculptural fragments in late fifth-century style are displayed in the British Museum.

Bassae carries on the architectural development we have seen on the Acropolis: in fact, as Pausanias tells us it was designed by Ictinos, architect of the Parthenon, it may well be a direct continuation of his work in Athens. Ictinos was pleased to push the rules in Athens; in Bassae they are pushed even further.

The temple is outwardly Doric, in a plain and rather unrefined style. The exterior suits its dedication to a soldier god, Apollo Epikourios, and suits its magnificent but bleak setting in bare mountain terrain. The building material is the sombre local limestone with a strange, fissured surface. Maybe it originally had a protective covering of marble stucco to lighten it up and keep the bad weather away. Sculptural detail was carried out in marble. The tiled roof was also of marble, as we know from Pausanias.

The building

There were six façade columns and fifteen to the flanks, an elongated, archaic proportion (Fig. 75). At 14.5 x 38.25 metres, the temple is not very large and refinements are minimal. There seems to be no upward curvature of the stylobate; if there is slight entasis of the Doric columns, it is almost imperceptible. On the two short ends, the columns are slightly thicker than those on the flanks: those on the flanks are spaced slightly more closely than those on the ends. These are archaic traits.

The two porches in antis are deep, the door of the pronaos being almost on a level with the fifth column, and the opisthodomos slightly shallower. This arrangement resembles that of the Hephaisteion (Fig. 69).

There was apparently no sculpture on the exterior metopes; it is uncertain whether there was any on the pediments, since they are shallow.

74. The temple of Apollo Epikourios at Bassae, *c.* 420 BC.

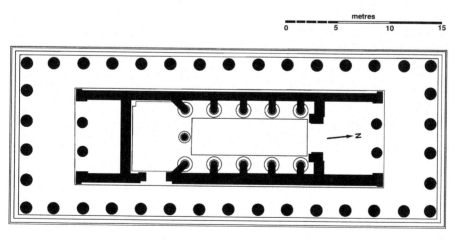

75. Ground plan of the temple of Apollo Epikourios.

76. Interior reconstruction by C.R. Cockerell of the temple of Apollo Epikourios looking towards the adyton. The ceiling is almost certainly incorrect.

Surprisingly, on the sloping cornices of the pediments was a beautiful carved anthemion: Doric temples routinely had painted patterns on cornices, but carved borders were an Ionic feature. This oddity hinted at the richness to be found on the interior.

14. The sanctuary of Apollo Epikourios at Bassae

Figural sculpture started on the inner porches, as at Olympia. The porch metopes contained scenes possibly depicting themes of departure and arrival: in the entrance porch, the return of Apollo in Spring from the land of the Hyperboreans; on the back porch, the departure of the Daughters of Leucippus, seized by the Dioscuri. If these interpretations are correct, the theme of arrival and departure would be particularly relevant to the sun-god in his daily and yearly cycle: in this harsh landscape of long winters, the return of spring must be especially welcome. Arrival and departure are also of keen interest to the professional soldier, especially as ancient warfare was seasonal, ceasing for the winter.

So far, the temple mainly follows the Doric formula, but with a certain archaism. One oddity is the north/south orientation with the main entrance facing north. Inside are two interconnecting chambers, the cella and a further small adyton. (It is the existence of this adyton which has demanded the fifteen flank columns – as at Delphi.) From this small chamber, a side entrance opens onto the eastern colonnade. This means that despite the odd north/south orientation, the rising sun can still strike into the temple.

The cella

In the cella are several surprises (Fig. 76). The interior colonnade is Ionic in two rows of five; each row is attached to its side-wall by short spur walls. It is now thought that this oddity preserves an earlier plan. (We have, for example, seen spur walls in the archaic temple of Hera at Olympia.) However, no columns have quite looked like these before. The capitals are Ionic, with rather heavy and widely spreading capitals of a unique design, which, unlike usual Ionic capitals, shows volutes on three sides. The reconstruction shows why this was necessary, given the sharp angle of viewing. The shafts are not made up of real drums, but of shaped sections which tie into the cella walls (Fig. 77). From the front, they resemble complete columns, but from the side, the rounded fluted section merges with an unfluted straight spur-wall. At the base, they swing out into large, rather flattened bases. (The swinging profile of these bases is an exaggerated version, reminiscent of the more conventional ones of Athene Nike on the Acropolis.) The bases are almost complete disks, interrupted only at the rear where the connecting spur joins the column to the wall. An advantage arises from the use of semi-engaged Ionic columns, even such strange ones as these. The tall thin proportion makes them 'space-savers', as they were in the Parthenon opisthodomus. Here there is an even greater need to save space, as this cella is really small. The use of engaged 'columns' – instead of two free-standing colonnades – makes the tiny area spatially viable as well as interesting with its unusual deep alcoves.

These columns are Ionic in a Doric building, a combination already familiar from the Parthenon and Propylaia, but here their peculiar forms

77. Interior of the temple of Apollo Epikourios.

arouse an additional feeling of strangeness and disorientation. The ancient viewer, looking towards the adyton and the eastern side-doorway, would have been astonished to see a limestone shaft blocking the way between the cella and the adyton and, on it, in glimmering white marble and colourful paint, a completely new kind of capital. This was the first

Corinthian capital that we know of, maybe the first in architecture (Fig. 76). Its particular suitability to the free-standing position is that the design of the four-sided capital works well from every direction.

The two Ionic end spur-columns towards the south – which flank and frame the Corinthian central column – are set at an angle. This can best be understood by reference to the plan (Fig. 75). Opinions differ as to whether these too were Corinthian, but it seems unlikely and would spoil the impact of the unique new-comer. This special column would have appeared differently according to whether the eastern door was letting in light. When illuminated, the adyton would show the silhouetted column up as dark, but if the cella was the only lit area, the column would stand out clearly against the dark adyton.

Sadly, the new capital was mysteriously destroyed, leaving only fragments and a sketch that was made on the day of discovery in the early nineteenth century AD. But the slim pale base is still to be seen in situ (Fig. 77), contrasting suggestively with its gloomy surroundings and with the wide plate-like bases of the Ionic columns. Callimachos, the sculptor who created the elaborate lamp cover 'like a palm tree' in the Erechtheum, has been suggested as the probable designer of the elaborately decorative new capital.

The frieze

The engaged colonnade of five Ionic flanking columns each side and one central Corinthian column supported an interior entablature and frieze. As far as we know, this is a 'first', maybe induced by a factor as prosaic as the bad weather-conditions outside, or maybe a natural step on from the semi-interior frieze of the Parthenon, or both. The frieze features an Amazonomachy and a Centauromachy. Apollo himself appears, with his twin sister Artemis, in a chariot drawn by deer. Together they pursue enemies round the walls – Lapiths fight Centaurs – Heracles is there too, taking the belt of the Queen of the Amazons (Fig. 78).

78. Interior frieze, temple of Apollo Epikourios, from section above Corinthian column. Heracles takes the belt of the Amazon queen.

155

Opinions differ greatly about the frieze. Some critics find it heavy and provincial; to others it is rich and exciting. The figure style is stocky, perhaps. But the action is dynamic. Drapery is more than wind-blown – it writhes with a life of its own – or it stretches taut between the sturdy thighs of fighting women. Each group is linked to the next by flailing limbs, cloaks or rearing horse-bodies.

Critics say that the frieze would have been invisible in the darkness of the interior: but it seems likely that oil lamps would have been suspended to illuminate it: a flickering light would have made the shadowed limbs and drapery seem to flutter and move. The relief is very deep, especially compared with the shallow Parthenon frieze. The composition is compact, lacking space but taking great advantage of depth. As Fig. 78 shows, there would be a strong **chiaroscuro** which would have been especially effective in artificial light. This frieze is harsher and harder than the Acropolis sculptures, but it seems appropriate to its mountain setting and its soldier deity. It would have made a powerful impression in the small-scale cella.

Dating the temple

Scholars were puzzled by many factors when it came to dating the temple. The dullness of the exterior, its north-south orientation, its archaic proportion and its odd side-door made some ask whether the temple itself was in truth archaic with an updated cella decor. But, it is now believed that this temple is simply based on its predecessors on the site. In fact archaic foundations have been excavated here with all the same oddities of layout: the length, the adyton, the eastern side-opening, the interior spur columns: so the fifth-century designer combined tradition with modernity. This conclusion leaves Pausanias' start-date of 430-429 perfectly persuasive, with sculpture probably completed by about 425 (although some have dated it as late as 390 on stylistic grounds).

Aesthetically, the cella creates a thrill of difference by contrast with the plain exterior. Why is it so wild? Is it because the remoteness allowed Ictinos a free hand for experiment? Or did the city committee ask for a cutting-edge design? This seems a bit unlikely – till we notice the fourth-century temple of Tegea, also in Arcadia, and even more experimental. Tegea was designed by the sculptor Skopas who ran with the idea of interior Corinthian columns, used a central eastern side door, and also introduced extreme emotion to Greek sculpture.

The statue

It is not clear whether there was a cult statue in the temple of Apollo. There may be some evidence of a statue base in the south-west corner of the adyton. In this case, the statue would have received the light of the rising sun, guided by the careful placement of the eastern opening; but would not have been clearly visible from the cella, or the main entrance. Pausanias mentions a twelve-foot-high bronze statue of Apollo Epikourios, which was moved from Bassae to Megalopolis where he saw it displayed 'in front of the precinct ... to help ornament the Great City' (Pausanias 8.xxx.3). This sounds like an exterior work rather than a cult statue, which would need to be inside the temple. There are some sculptural fragments of a large **acrolithic** (i.e. with only the hands, feet and face of stone) statue from the temple, but they are thought to be Hellenistic or Roman and not original to the design. The central column in any case gave rise to the problem faced by the earliest temples with their central colonnades: it rather interfered with a satisfactory placement of a cult statue. To place the statue centrally either in front of, or behind, the column would be a pity, as the one would obscure the other. One intriguing suggestion is that the central column took the place of a statue, and its slender shaft and foliage-like capital represented the elegant long-haired god himself.

Apollo Epikourios

'Apollo the Helper': according to Pausanias, Apollo received this title for his help in stopping the plague of 430 or 420. However, as it can be seen that the sanctuary itself is far older than the present temple, other explanations have been sought for the name. *Epikouros* can have the specific meaning of 'mercenary soldier', and the tough mountain men traditionally added to their meagre living by following this profession. They might have adopted Apollo as their patron specifically for this activity, or simply as their helper and ally generally; and the name could be as old as the sanctuary. Many finds of votive offerings of specially made miniature bronze armour back a military view of the cult at Bassae. Apollo as concerned with soldiers is unexpected but not unique, and fits the needs of the people who worshipped him here.

Phigaleia was the polis which built the sanctuary. Even for the people of Phigaleia, the temple was remote and hard to reach; only a long hard trek from the city would bring the worshipper to the dramatic goal. Judging from the harshness of temperature even in spring, the winter must have made it largely unviable and snow-bound. How welcome the return of the sun-god from the land of the Hyperboreans!

Pausanias tells us that Ictinos designed the temple (Pausanias 8.xli.9). This information might seem a bit far-fetched – but the temple shows signs of similarity with the Parthenon. There is the willingness to experiment and to find new solutions to fit the specific brief. There is the mix of orders. (This is the first known building to include all three.) There is the Ionic frieze – and intriguingly, it quotes the Parthenon sculpture: Heracles and the Amazon queen adopt the same chiastic pose as that of Athene and Poseidon on the west pediment (Figs 44, 78). The quotation could act as a sort of signature.

Pericles had his enemies – and we know that they attacked him through Pheidias, engineering the sculptor's exile from Athens (and resulting incidentally in the commission for the great Zeus of Olympia). It may be that Ictinos too found it convenient to accept work far away from Athens. If so, we can see that at least his exile did not cramp his creativity.

15

Looking at art in sanctuaries

How did the ancient viewer look at art and architecture? We have made some guesses from the evidence of the art itself. A few scattered clues can be found in literature too. For example, there is one unusual extended dramatic passage worth examining, as it represents the 'public' in the act of looking at art in a sanctuary.

A visit to Delphi is featured in Euripides' play, *Ion* (mentioned in Chapter 11). Queen Creusa, daughter of Erechtheus, has come from Athens with her husband King Xouthos to consult the oracle about their childlessness. Creusa also has a secret sorrow: as a young girl she was raped by Apollo, and the resulting baby she bore in secret and hid in a cave under the Acropolis. That baby disappeared and, without her knowledge, has been brought to Delphi by the god Hermes: it is Ion, now the young temple-servant.

Towards the beginning of the play is a scene (Euripides, *Ion* 200-50) in which the Chorus of women from Athens are looking around at the various buildings and sculptures; they are the slaves of Queen Creusa. They are normal visitors, not in any sense art-experts. These women are having a wonderful time (in contrast to their poor mistress who is suffering heart-break). Their first response to the sanctuary is to compare it with what they already know:

> Not in holy Athens only
> Are there finely columned temples
> Or worship of Apollo who guards the streets.
> At the shrine of Loxias also,
> Son of Leto, from twin faces
> Shines the light of lovely eyes.

They note two architectural features at Delphi – colonnades and pediments – which are standard and which they relate with pleasure to their experience at home. The expression 'light of lovely eyes' assures us that their response to the new building is positive.

Having briefly noted the basic architectural points, their interest is caught by sculptured myths. They examine what might be a series of metopes including 'Heracles killing the Hydra'. Their method is to keep looking till they can identify all the details, including the hero's faithful companion, Iolaos, 'whose story is told to us at our looms'. Their pleasure is in finding, in an unfamiliar place, familiar stories already associated with their daily routine. And they enjoy the process of identification. The more clue-giving details there are, the better. They also respond to the story-telling skill of the sculptor since they use heightened vocabulary to describe the scenes, such as 'blazing ... fire-breathing ... terrible double-flaming ... burns up with fire ...': they find these sculpted narratives not only life-like but exciting.

As a group, they pick out figures from the Gigantomachy which probably featured on the rear of Apollo's temple. They are all the more delighted with it because this same scene was on several Acropolis buildings, especially the east metopes of the Parthenon. In the Athenian telling of this story, it was Athene who did remarkable deeds.

> Do you see her shake her shield,
> her Gorgon-faced shield over giant Enceladus?
> – I see Athene, my own goddess!

These enjoyable stories also involve personal and Greek identity. The women have left their home, but they are still in Greece and – to that extent – at home. Athene is their goddess and she is here too.

Next, the women ask the guide, Ion, a typical tourist question:

> *Chorus*: Does Phoebus' temple truly stand
> on the navel-centre of the earth?
> *Ion*: Yes, dressed in garlands, Gorgons all around.
> *Chorus*: Just what we've always heard!

As typical tourists they are happy to be given the kind of information they expected, and happy to look at 'what is allowed.' Since they may not go into the temple itself without the sacrifice of a sheep, they will enjoy 'looking round outside'. When Creusa, their royal mistress, joins them, Ion notices that her behaviour is very untypical: 'The sight of Apollo's sanctuary has made you weep! ... Everyone else is happy when they gaze at the god's house, but you – your eyes run with tears.' Creusa of course has special issues with Apollo – her rape and the loss of her baby – but the normal 'worshipper' finds positive enjoyment in the experience of seeing a temple building.

The Chorus of women does not distinguish between what is religious, aesthetic, cultural or social. All these experiences are wrapped up together. They enjoy the leisure of the visit, the display of art, the expression of Greekness and the unseen presence of Apollo. This is a day out, a holiday, and there is something for everyone.

Euripides has employed an unusual method of scene-setting for his drama, by using the spontaneous comments of the Chorus on art. He has surely made it as plausible as possible, reflecting the kind of comments really made by the general public: their main interest is clearly in story-identification and in relating what they see to previous experience. There is also throughout the scene an emphasis on simple enjoyment and pleasure in the experience of visiting a shrine: this would be applicable to all the sanctuaries we have looked at.

Conclusion

The sanctuaries examined in this book are particularly famous. It is hoped that, by looking in some detail at the buildings contained in them, the reader has acquired, pleasurably and without too much trouble, a wide range of architectural vocabulary and concepts. It should be possible to build on this knowledge in many ways. The elements of architecture and architectural ornament are all around us in our built environment, or may be sought out in specialised museums. The sites themselves may be visited, or others like them. I hope that the student of ancient architecture will find that further study has been made easier by this introduction.

Further reading

Ashmole, B., *Architect and Sculptor in Classical Greece* (Phaidon, 1972)

Barletta, B., *The Origins of the Greek Architectural Orders* (Cambridge University Press, 2001)

Buitron-Oliver, D. (ed.), *The Interpretation of Architectural Sculpture in Greece and Rome*. Studies in the History of Art, 49. Center for Advanced Study in the Visual Arts, Symposium Papers XXIX (Hanover and London, 1997)

Coulton, J.J., *Ancient Greek Architects at Work* (Cornell University Press, 1977)

Dinsmoor, W.B. *The Architecture of Ancient Greece*, 3rd edn (W.W. Norton, 1975)

Ekonomakis, R. (ed.), *Acropolis Restoration: The CCAM Interventions* (Academy Editions, 1994)

Hurwit, J.M., *The Art and Culture of Early Greece, 1100-480 BC* (Cornell University Press, 1985)

Hurwit, J.M., *The Athenian Acropolis: History, Mythology and Archaeology from the Neolithic Era to the Present* (Cambridge University Press, 1999)

Hurwit, J.M., *The Acropolis in the Age of Pericles* (Cambridge University Press, 2004)

Korres, M., *From Pentelicon to the Parthenon* (Melissa, 1995)

Lagerlof, M.R., *The Sculptures of the Parthenon: Aesthetics and Interpretation* (Yale University Press, 2000)

Lawrence, A.W., *Greek Architecture*, fifth edn, rev. R.A. Tomlinson (Yale University Press, 1996)

Neils, J., *The Parthenon Frieze* (Cambridge University Press, 2001)

Pausanias, *Guide to Greece*, vols 1 & 2, trans. Peter Levi (Penguin, 1979)

Pedley, J., *Sanctuaries and the Sacred in the Ancient Greek World* (Cambridge University Press, 2005)

Rhodes, R.F., *Architecture and Meaning on the Athenian Acropolis* (Cambridge University Press, 1995)

Ridgway, B.S., *Prayers in Stone, Greek Architectural Sculpture (c. 600-100 BCE)* (University of California Press, 1999)

Sinn, U., *Olympia: Cult, Sport and Ancient Festival* (Max Weiner, 2001)

Valavanis, P., *Games and Sanctuaries in Ancient Greece* (J.P. Getty Museum, 2004)

Woodford, S., *The Parthenon* (Cambridge University Press, 1981)

Glossary

abacus – square member of a Doric capital, just above the echinus and below the architrave; also used in Ionic and Corinthian but with concave sides.

acanthus – frequently used design motif based on the acanthus thistle leaf.

acrolithic – type of statue where only head, arms and feet are of stone, with a wooden body.

acroterion – sculptural flourish, floral or figurative, topping the three corners of a pediment.

adyton – innermost chamber of a temple.

aegis – a garment worn only by Athene, resembling a poncho worn centrally or sometimes asymmetrically over the shoulders. It is edged with snakes and may have a Gorgoneion (Gorgon's head) in the centre. Its function is to protect friends and terrify enemies.

Agora – civic centre, similar to the Roman Forum.

amphiprostyle – prostyle façade on both back and front of a building.

anathyrosis – smooth worked band on masonry intended to fit perfectly with adjacent masonry. The rest is cut slightly deeper so as to require less exact work.

aniconic – non-representational.

anta/antae – projection of side wall beyond a corner; or decorative pilaster marking termination of a side wall.

antefix – repeated terracotta or marble ornament covering the lowest tile ends of a roof.

anthemion – floral border design, same as lotus-and-palmette.

anulet – thin ring around the top of a Doric column shaft – 'necking ring'.

apse – rounded end to a building.

architrave – 'main beam' lying on top of colonnade and supporting entablature and roof.

arris – the sharp edge of the flutes on a Doric column.

ashlar masonry – regular courses of blocks cut to neat rectangles.

base of a column – absent in Doric style; in Ionic can be quite elaborate.

bead-and-reel – moulding design (see Fig. 12).

capital – the decorative top member of a column; indicates its 'order'.

caryatids – architectural term for columns in the form of women.

cella – main chamber of a temple; also called naos.

chiaroscuro – artistic effect of dark and light.

chiton – Ionic dress of elaborately folded and pinned cloth.

chryselephantine – sculpture made with gold and ivory plates on a wooden core.

coffering – method of making a decorative ceiling, using diminishing square steps like boxes; either marble or wood.

Corinthian – decorative order of architecture: capitals have small volutes and bands of acanthus foliage running underneath, otherwise similar to Ionic; first noted at Bassae.

cornice – a protruding section like a frame above a wall or surrounding a pediment; both decorative and protective.

cult-statue – statue focusing devotion in a particular cult: fixed focal statue in a temple.

Cyclopean – Mycenaean-age wall construction named after giants, consisting of massive boulders fitted quite roughly together with small stones filling gaps.

demos – the people; 'democracy' = rule of the people.

dentils – design of small square blocks alternating with spaces, an Ionic feature.

dipteral – a temple with a double colonnade all round.

distyle in antis – arrangement of porch columns where two columns stand between the antae or short spur walls, the normal Doric arrangement; see Fig 3.

Doric – plain order of architecture, mainly used on mainland Greece; see Fig. 2.

Doric frieze – horizontal element above the architrave; divided into triglyphs and metopes.

dressed stone – masonry neatly cut to shape on the front face.

drum – cylindrical section of a column, or any cylindrical form.

echinus – literally 'cushion': simple rounded member, characteristic part of a Doric capital; or small equivalent at top of an Ionic capital.

egg-and-dart – moulding design (see Fig. 12).

Eleusinian marble/limestone – dark stone from Eleusis, used for colour contrast.

entablature – entire superstructure supported by columns: or architrave + frieze + cornice.

entasis – subtle curve of columns.

fillet – narrow flat strip; used of flat member between Ionic flutes.

flute, fluting – vertical decorative channels on columns.

frieze – horizontal member above the architrave; may or may not be sculpted.

guilloche – a plaited moulding design (see Fig. 65).

guttae – small decorative knobs found under Doric mutules; they resemble wooden pegs.

hexastyle – façade or inner porch with six columns.

hipped roof – roof sloping on four sides, without gables or pediments.

in antis – describes arrangement of porch columns between the antae.

intercolumniation – distance between columns in a colonnade.

Ionic – decorative order of architecture originating in eastern Greece; see Fig. 4.

Ionic frieze – continuous 'ribbon' frieze found above the architrave; may or may not be sculpted.

island marble – marble imported from islands, usually Naxos or Paros.

kore (plural **korai**) – archaic statue type of a standing maiden, often holding an offering.

kouros (plural **kouroi**) – archaic statue type of a nude youth stepping forward with clenched hands held close to his sides.

limestone – cheap stone, usually local; related to marble but much coarser.

lintel – horizontal beam spanning a door frame or supported on columns.

lotus-and-palmette – floral moulding design (see Fig. 12).

metope – rectangular or square flat section between triglyphs; can be painted, plain or sculpted.

monolithic – made of a single piece of stone.

moulding – decorative carved border.

mutules – flat blocks decorated on the underside with guttae found under the Doric cornice.

Naxian – marble from Naxos; tends to be greyer and more loosely crystalline than Parian.

Nike (plural **Nikai**) – Victory or winged figure of victory.

numinous – place emanating a natural impression of a spiritual presence.

octostyle – façade or inner porch with eight columns.

opisthodomos – rear porch of a temple; sometimes a back-chamber.

orthostates – upright slabs forming the lowest course of a wall; usually double the height of the subsequent courses.

palaistra – peristyle building used for athletic and other educational activities.

Parian – marble from the island of Paros; pure, translucent white marble.

Pentelic marble – marble quarried in Attica from M Pentelicon; the marble of choice for Athenians from the second quarter of the fifth century onwards; very fine texture and warm colouring.

peplos – long dress made of folded and pinned rectangle of cloth. A plain mainland style.

peribolos – wall surrounding a temenos.

peripteral – temple with colonnade running all round exterior.

peristyle – outer colonnade of a temple; sometimes inner colonnade of a courtyard building.

phiale (plural **phialai**) – flat libation dish, either plain or lobed.

pier – squared column or pillar.

pilaster – flat squared or half-round column, stuck to wall.

polis – city-state.

polygonal – irregular but closely fitting masonry style; particularly used in earthquake zones.

poros – a type of stone; a word sometimes used generally for limestone.

pronaos – front porch of a temple.

propylaia – a more elaborate propylon.

propylon – monumental gateway.

prostyle – arrangement of façade columns where colonnade stretches right across platform.

pteroma – corridor between colonnade and cella walls of a temple.

pteron – flank colonnade of a temple (i.e. not the front or back porch).

reeded – carved with horizontal grooves or convex flutes.

refinements – system of deliberate deviations from straight lines for optical effects.

regulae – same as mutules.

riser – vertical part of a step.

rosette – flat circular flower-shaped decoration.

scotia – concave section between two toruses on an Ionic column-base (see Fig. 65).

shelly limestone – a local limestone found near Olympia with a loose texture owing to its fossilised shell content.

sima – a gutter, often highly decorative, edging a roof where the slope meets the walls.

soffit – horizontal element masking the underside of the roof overhang. Sometimes decorated.

stereobate – the three-stepped platform of a temple.

stoa – roofed building with open colonnaded front.

stucco – a lime-plaster, to protect mud-brick walls, or mixed with marble dust, to mask the impurities of limestone and make it look like marble.

stylobate – platform on which columns sit; top step of a stereobate.
symposium – dinner party.
tainia – 'garland': a thin projecting band along the top of a Doric architrave.
temenos – designated sacred area.
tetrastyle – façade or inner porch with four columns.
tholos – circular building.
torus – cushion-like member of an Ionic column-base or convex moulding (see Fig. 65).
tread – flat part of a step.
triglyph – slab with three vertical grooves, part of Doric frieze, alternates with metopes.
tripteral – temple surrounded by three colonnades.
tympanum – the vertical triangular wall of a pediment, against which sculpture stands.
volute – scroll ornament found on Ionic columns and door-frames.
xystos – running track covered by colonnaded roof.

Index

Index

CPSIA information can be obtained
at www.ICGtesting.com
Printed in the USA
LVOW01s2000130616

492409LV00003B/7/P

9 781853 996894